the knot
ultimate
wedding
planner

ALSO BY THE KNOT

The Knot Complete Guide to Weddings

The Knot Ultimate Wedding Planner Binder

The Knot Ultimate Wedding Lookbook

The Knot Guide to Destination Weddings

The Knot Guide to Wedding Vows and Traditions

The Knot Book of Wedding Lists

the knot
ultimate
wedding
planner

Worksheets, checklists, etiquette, timelines, and answers to frequently asked questions

carley roney
and the editors of TheKnot.com

CLARKSON POTTER/PUBLISHERS
NEW YORK

Published in the United States by Clarkson Potter/Publishers, an imprint of the
Crown Publishing Group, a division of Random House, Inc., New York.
www.crownpublishing.com
www.clarksonpotter.com

CLARKSON POTTER is a trademark and POTTER with colophon is a registered
trademark of Random House, Inc.

A previous edition of this work was published in the United States by Broadway
Books, an imprint of the Crown Publishing Group, a division of Random House, Inc.,
New York, in 1999.

Library of Congress Cataloging-in-Publication Data
Roney, Carley.
   The Knot ultimate wedding planner / Carley Roney and the editors of
TheKnot.com. — 1st rev. ed.
      p.   cm.
      1. Weddings—Planning.   2. Wedding etiquette.   I. Knot (Firm).   II. Title.
III. Title: Knot ultimate wedding planner.
   HQ45.R65   2012
   395.2'2—dc23   2012024633

ISBN 978-0-7704-3377-2
eISBN 978-0-7704-3381-9

Printed in the United States of America

Front cover photographs (clockwise from top left): Creative Heirloom Photography;
Sofia Negron Photography; Jasmine Star Photography; Harwell Photography; Kate
Mathis; Antonis Achilleos; Jen Kroll Photography; Mary Wyar Photography

Back cover photographs (left to right): KT Merry Photography, Janae Shields
Photography; Pen/Carlson; Adam Barnes Fine Art Photography • Author photograph:
Troy House

10

First Revised Edition

contents

getting started

HOW TO USE THIS BOOK

Planning a wedding involves endless details, pressing deadlines, family drama, and—far too often—enough stress to make you want to just elope. *The Knot Ultimate Wedding Planner* is a couple's secret weapon against such insanity. It's your cheat sheet—telling you what you need to know and do, and when. It's your insider's guide—giving you the most essential expert advice from TheKnot.com in bite-size, easy-to-follow steps. It's your security blanket—the next-best thing to a guarantee that you'll have a memorable wedding while maintaining a handle on unwarranted stress.

envision your wedding day style
Before you get overwhelmed by all those to-dos, sit down together and read chapter 1, "Finding Your Style." The worksheets at the start of each chapter will help you focus your thoughts, decide exactly what kind of wedding you want to have, and create a vision for each and every detail. As you're filling each one out, keep an open mind; your answers will help inform future wedding detail decisions. You'll also need to finalize a budget before you put down a single deposit—our easy worksheet on page 35 will lead you through it.

make a plan
We devoted the entire second chapter to what will become your wedding planning bible—from your overall calendar to a coordinating checklist that lays out the entire process and tells you what to do when. We know you want to get right into the fun stuff, like choosing colors and finding a dress, but before you lose yourself in the details, read this chapter all the way through to get a sense of the timing and steps involved. To personalize your calendar, count back from your wedding date and fill in the actual deadlines: one month before, two months before, and so on.

do your wedding vendor homework

Once you have an idea of what you're looking for, you'll need to find professionals to handle the task. Read wedding vendor reviews online, ask recently married friends for recommendations, and don't hire anyone until you've asked each and every question on the lists in each chapter. Vendors' answers will clue you in to how they approach their work—and to whether their approach is appropriate for your wedding.

read the expert planning tips

In each chapter, we share wedding planning essentials—what we've learned in our years of experience talking to wedding professionals and hundreds of thousands of couples. Read these essential tips and money-saving tricks; then, before you make any final decisions, peruse the "Ask Carley" sections for up-to-date answers to the most frequently asked questions in each category. For our comprehensive advice—and unlimited ideas—get a copy of our companion reference, the 450-page *The Knot Complete Guide to Weddings*, and, of course, you'll want to sign up for free as a member of TheKnot.com, where you can create your own wedding website, browse thousands of real wedding photos, research wedding vendors in your area, manage your guest list, and stay up-to-date on the latest wedding news. We'll even send you weekly e-mails to keep you on track if you want.

keep track of wedding details

The latter part of each chapter gets into the specifics of executing your plan. Use our checklists to make sure your contract with each vendor is complete. Fill out a cheat sheet for each professional you hire—you'll need easy access to their information as other vendors request it or when it's needed in an emergency. (Hint: Attach the vendors' business cards to their respective contact pages.)

personalize our tips

This book is about realistic guidelines, not hard-and-fast rules. Feel free to adjust the process according to your own priorities. If photography means everything to you, by all means spend 12 percent of your budget on your package instead of the suggested 10 percent (just make sure the total wedding budget still adds up to 100 percent). Same goes for etiquette: We give you the guidelines, but it's up to you to apply them.

have fun (seriously!)

It's true: Planning a wedding can be a roller-coaster ride. But considering this is likely to be the most extravagant party you'll ever throw in your lives, you'd better have a blast—from your first hour brainstorming all the way through to the last five seconds of your reception. We'll help, of course, but here's some general advice: Don't drive yourself crazy over every single detail. Declare some days wedding-planning-free. And most of all, keep your perspective and remember the reason you're planning this wedding (you're getting married!).

ASK CARLEY

getting started

I've got this book, but what else do I need?

Planning a wedding is all about staying organized. You need shortcuts, easy access to your info, and quick ways to plan while you multitask. First, download The Knot Ultimate Planner App to your phone. You'll have access to your checklist, vendor contacts, guest list, budgeter, and all of your saved photos wherever you go. You'll also want to link your registry to your phone. That way, you can add that comforter to the list the minute you see it. If you're an uber-planner and superexcited to share all the details, you might also want to start a planning blog (Wordpress.com has some really cute templates). Speaking of sharing all the details, make sure you have an easy way to gather all of the photos that your friends and family take at the wedding. Create a hashtag for your wedding (and spread the news via your wedding website) or have guests tag them to your Facebook or wedding album. Honestly, the options are ever-changing—but we keep a close eye on all the cool tools available—so find quick links for our favorite wedding planning apps at TheKnot.com/apps.

How do I even begin to navigate all of the wedding info online?

Simply put, there are three major tasks you're going to tackle online.

1. Save your favorite photos. Planning a wedding is extremely visual. As you begin to browse all those gorgeous photos, you'll start to really hone in on what you like stylistically and color-wise. Keep those images all together in one spot for quick reference when you're meeting with the florist and stationer (to ensure you're both talking about the same thing when you say "romantic" or "light purple").

2. Find your vendors. Yes, you should ask recently married friends for recommendations, but you'll also have to do your homework online. Start with basic search phrases like "Wedding Florist in Chicago" or "Los Angeles Wedding Reception Venues." Check out prospective vendor websites and look for photos from recent events. If you like what you see, get in touch and set up an informational call or meeting.

3. Read reviews. Crowd-sourced knowledge is the best way to get the inside scoop and ensure you've found the right person for the job. If you can't find one review, that's a red flag. Several bad reviews in a row is obviously also a bad sign. As you're reading, look for similarities among the reviews (for example, if five different people said that everyone raved about the food or that it was always easy to get in touch with the vendor) to really understand what it's like to work with this person or company.

notes

_____
_____
_____
_____
_____
_____
_____
_____
_____
_____
_____
_____
_____

Cara & Stephen
RUSTIC MEETS GLAM
MAY 29
MANAHAWKIN, NJ

Cara and Stephen
wanted a wedding near
the beach without an
overly beachy theme. The
rustic boathouse chapel
ultimately sold them.
They took a modern
approach to the décor
and incorporated lots of
bright colors and metallic
accents such as a glittery
gold aisle runner, and
the cake—decorated
with sugar flowers—was
wrapped, ombré-style,
in colorful bands.

finding your style

Once you announce your upcoming wedding, everyone in the
world will have opinions for you. Before that happens, make sure
you spend some time together—just the two of you—trying to
discover your own wedding style. Be clear right from the start as to
who will be involved in making decisions and how the tasks of
planning will be divided. Brace yourself for a little inevitable family
drama. But most of all, enjoy yourselves in these early weeks: Use
the excuse to go out and celebrate (often!) with friends.

your wedding style worksheet

Chances are you have some vision of what your wedding will be like.
Sit down and fill out this worksheet together (or make a copy for each
of you so your answers aren't skewed).

describe the event (check all that apply)

☐ Grand   ☐ Glamorous   ☐ Festive   ☐ Destination
☐ Formal   ☐ Modern   ☐ Fun   ☐ Seasonal
☐ Refined   ☐ Vintage   ☐ Offbeat   ☐ Ethnic
☐ Elegant   ☐ Relaxed   ☐ Rustic   ☐ Religious
☐ Romantic   ☐ Intimate   ☐ Vineyard   ☐ Other _____
☐ Classic   ☐ Casual   ☐ Beach

where you want to have it

☐ Where you live   ☐ Where your   ☐ Where your fiancé's   ☐ Somewhere far away
                     parents live   family lives   (destination wedding)

ideal size

☐ Intimate (<100)   ☐ Average (100–200)   ☐ Large (200–350)   ☐ Immense! (350+)

Approx. # of guests _____

ideal season

☐ Spring/Summer   ☐ Fall/Winter

exact month (if you already have one in mind) _____

ideal wedding date 1st _____ / _____ / _____   2nd _____ / _____ / _____

ideal ceremony hour

☐ Sunrise   ☐ Evening   ☐ Sunset
☐ Midday   ☐ Late-night

ideal time of day 1st _____   2nd _____

favorite color palette (check all that apply)

☐ Bright and bold   ☐ Rich jewel tones   ☐ Metallics/neutrals   ☐ Citrus colors
☐ All (or mostly) white   ☐ Soft pastels   ☐ Earth tones   ☐ Seasonal colors
☐ Black with an accent

☐ Specific colors _____

parties you need to plan (beyond the reception) (check all that apply)

☐ Engagement party   ☐ Rehearsal dinner   ☐ After-party
☐ Bridesmaid luncheon   ☐ Welcome party   ☐ Postwedding brunch

your reception priorities (rank from 1 to 10)

_____ Time of year/day of week   _____ Reception setting (proximity or type)
_____ Officiant or ceremony location   _____ Wedding dress
_____ Guest list (big family, a large invite list)   _____ Ambience (flowers and décor)
_____ Food and drink   _____ Mementos (photo and video)
_____ Music (band and/or DJ)   _____ Other _____

opinions that count (check all that apply; asterisk [*] who has final word)

☐ You two   ☐ Friends and attendants   ☐ Your parents   ☐ Your fiancé's parents
☐ Other people _____

planning committee (check all that apply; asterisk [*] who is in charge)

☐ You two   ☐ Friends and attendants   ☐ Wedding coordinator
☐ Your parents   ☐ Your fiancé's parents
☐ Other people _____

Use this space to outline your perfect wedding. Sit down together and write words that describe the wedding you want to have. Anything goes here!

_____

_____

_____

_____

_____

_____

_____

timeline & budget

do you need a wedding planner?

A wedding planner will help you search for the perfect venue and find great vendors that will fit within your planning budget. (In fact, a successful planner will have relationships with vendors that will often allow him to negotiate deals you wouldn't be able to get on your own.)

what type of wedding planner?

☐ Full-service designer and planner (styles and plans)

☐ Full-service planner

☐ Designer and month-of coordinator

☐ Month-of coordinator

☐ "Blueprint" planner (provides design ideas, you execute the plans)

your wedding planner budget $ _____

Julie & Bill
OUTDOOR ROMANCE
NOVEMBER 21
RANCHO PALOS
VERDES, CA

Julie had a vision, but because of her busy job, she hired a wedding planner to help pull it off. The result? A simple ceremony beneath a wooden pergola along the water. The color palette transitioned from clean all-white on the bluffs to deep, rich jewel tones with an emphasis on wines and plums (and lots of lush florals) in a romantic ballroom.

questions to ask
wedding planners

Is he or she available on your wedding date?

_____

_____

What's his or her typical price range?

_____

_____

What's the cost of the average wedding he or she plans?

_____

_____

What sorts of services does he or she offer (day-of, event planning, partial planning, etc.)?

_____

_____

How long has he or she been a planner?

_____

_____

How many weddings does he or she plan a year?

_____

_____

What is the most unique wedding he or she has ever planned?

_____

_____

Does he or she handle vendor services, contracts, and payment processing? (Some planners will request a lump sum and from there handle hiring and paying for vendors for you. Others will ask you to cut the checks for vendors yourselves.)

_____

_____

Does he or she create the overall vision, or is he or she more of a producer who brings in an event designer? Does he or she handle event styling?

_____

_____

Does he or she handle guest list coordination and RSVPs?

_____

_____

Does he or she do destination weddings (if applicable)?

_____

_____

Does he or she handle rentals?

_____

_____

What is really his or her specialty—styling or coordinating? Does he or she do day-of coordination?

_____

_____

timeline & budget

planner contact cheat sheet

wedding planner

name _____

website _____

phone _____

e-mail _____

address _____

total cost $ _____

deposit $ _____   date paid _____

balance $ _____   date due _____

notes _____

_____

_____

staple business card here

hiring your wedding planner

- ☐ Book your planner. Send him an e-mail confirmation or get it in writing to ensure you have a paper trail.

- ☐ Request a contract and review for the following critical points:
  - ☐ Name and contact information for you and the planner
  - ☐ Date, times, and locations of your ceremony and reception
  - ☐ An itemized list of all the services you've booked the planner for
  - ☐ A list of anything the planner will supply or take care of

- ☐ Arrival times and time needed for setup at the ceremony and reception sites
- ☐ The names of the planners and assistants who will be on hand during the wedding
- ☐ Total cost
- ☐ Deposit amount due
- ☐ Balance and date due
- ☐ Cancellation and refund policy
- ☐ Planner's signature

- ☐ Sign the final contract.

timeline & budget

notes
_____
_____
_____
_____
_____
_____
_____
_____
_____
_____
_____
_____
_____
_____
_____

your wedding inspiration

Create your wedding inspiration board here. Add inspiring
photos, color swatches, details, and themes you love.

*attach inspiring
photos here!*

your planning timeline

This checklist will guide you through the major to-dos of planning a wedding. We've based it on a yearlong engagement. If you have more time, lucky you! Hire your high-priority professionals as early as you can (maybe it's an amazing photographer or a twelve-piece band), especially if they're in high demand. If you have less time, we've created a five-months-or-less express engagement checklist. See the relevant chapters (noted in parentheses) for more detailed breakdowns of your to-dos on each wedding topic.

wedding planning timeline

12+ months before (or ASAP)

- [ ] Announce your engagement and spread the word. After you've told your friends and family and changed your Facebook status, consider sending in a newspaper engagement announcement or even creating a cute "We're engaged!" video or photo announcement card.

- [ ] Get organized. Create a separate e-mail folder to keep all wedding-related communication and research together. Go to TheKnot.com/planner for easy access to all your online planning tools (inspiration board, checklist, budgeter).

- [ ] Envision your overall wedding style and colors. (Use the worksheet in chapter 1.)

- [ ] Draw up your wedding budget with help from your families. (Use the worksheet in chapter 3.)

- [ ] Have your engagement ring insured.

- [ ] Choose a wedding date and time.

- [ ] Outline the initial guest list. (See chapter 4.)

- [ ] Create your wedding website. (It's free at TheKnot.com/pwp.) Add your "how you met and got engaged" story and photos. Then update it with venue and hotel info later as you make your choices.

- [ ] Research reception and ceremony sites. (See chapters 9 and 15.)

- [ ] Book any priority vendors (that is, if you know there's a particular band or photographer you *have* to have).

- [ ] Interview and book a wedding planner. (See chapter 1.)

9–11 months before   by ___ /___

- [ ] Reserve your date at your house of worship, or start looking for a civil ceremony site. (See chapter 15.)

- [ ] Book your reception venue. (See chapter 9.)

- [ ] If a priest, minister, or rabbi at a house of worship isn't marrying you, choose and book an officiant.

- [ ] Having an engagement party? Set a date, draft a guest list, and order invites. (See chapter 8.)

- [ ] Choose your wedding party. Also consider roles for other very important friends and family (ceremony readers, guest book attendants, candle lighters). (See chapter 6.)

- [ ] Settle on wedding colors and style.

- [ ] Decide on a caterer and determine a rough price per head. Then start thinking about the reception menu. (See chapter 10.)

- [ ] Start shopping for a wedding dress. (See chapter 12.)

- [ ] Finalize your guest list.

- [ ] Research photographers and videographers in your area. (See chapters 17 and 18.)

- [ ] Start researching DJs and reception bands. (See chapter 19.)

- [ ] Picture your flowers; set up appointments with florists in the area to discuss options. (See chapter 20.)

- [ ] Research lighting and rental places in your area (if you're having an outdoor wedding or want to add a few extras).

6–8 months before   by ___ / ___

- [ ] Order your wedding dress. (See chapter 12.)
- [ ] Register for gifts. (See chapter 7.)
- [ ] Think about bridesmaid dresses and what you want them to look like.
- [ ] Plan out the ceremony with your officiant and talk about any religious requirements.
- [ ] Book your florist. (See chapter 20.)
- [ ] Book your photographer. (See chapter 17.)
- [ ] Book your videographer. (See chapter 18.)
- [ ] Book your reception band or DJ. (See chapter 19.)
- [ ] Have engagement photos taken (if you want).
- [ ] Start planning your honeymoon. (See chapter 22.)
- [ ] Research ceremony musicians and book the one you love. (See chapter 15.)
- [ ] Think about hairstyles and start researching hair and makeup artists. (See chapter 12.)
- [ ] Interview and book a cake baker you love. (See chapter 11.)
- [ ] Nail down your bridesmaid dress pick. (See chapter 13.)
- [ ] Prep for out-of-town guests and set aside a block of rooms at nearby hotels (put that info on your wedding website). (See chapter 6.)
- [ ] Order save-the-dates and send them out to all of your guests. (See chapter 5.)
- [ ] Plan the rehearsal dinner. (See chapter 8.)
- [ ] Order your invitations. (See chapter 5.)
- [ ] Finalize the menu with your caterer.
- [ ] Research wedding insurance.
- [ ] Figure out which centerpieces you like.

4–5 months before   by ___ / ___

- [ ] Finalize your flower proposal with your florist.
- [ ] Decide on formalwear. (See chapter 14.)
- [ ] Reserve a calligrapher (if you're using one).
- [ ] Finalize your rental list (tables, chairs, extras).
- [ ] If you're planning a welcome party, finalize the details.
- [ ] Make all honeymoon travel reservations.
- [ ] Address those invitations. (Send them at the 3-month mark.)
- [ ] Book your wedding-night accommodations.
- [ ] Book the rehearsal dinner site.
- [ ] Brainstorm the groom's cake design.

2–3 months before   by ___ / ___

- [ ] Choose accessories (shoes, jewelry) for your bridesmaids and confirm their dress deliveries.
- [ ] Decide on a marriage contract (*ketubah* or any other contract required) for the ceremony.
- [ ] Buy or rent the ceremony and reception decorations that aren't included in your flower proposal (aisle runner, program basket).
- [ ] Make all prewedding beauty appointments (facials, haircuts, color).
- [ ] Attend prewedding counseling (if required).
- [ ] Shop for and buy your wedding rings. (See chapter 15.)
- [ ] Send out wedding invites at the 3-month mark.

the knot TIP
Keep track of all these to-dos online (and set up reminders for yourself) at **TheKnot.com/checklist.**

timeline & budget

- ☐ Decide on wedding favors.

- ☐ If you're planning to host a bridesmaid luncheon, finalize the details and let your bridesmaids know.

- ☐ Arrange for day-of transportation for you, your wedding party, and your guests (if needed). (See chapter 16.)

- ☐ Confirm the delivery date of your dress and schedule your dress fittings.

- ☐ Purchase your under-the-dress essentials and shoes in time for your first fitting.

- ☐ Have your bridal shower.

- ☐ Figure out ceremony readings and reach out to the people you want involved.

- ☐ Work on the ceremony (chapter 15) and start writing your vows (if you're writing your own).

- ☐ Draw up reception song lists (including the must-play and do-not-play lists).

2 months before   by ___ /___

- ☐ Start working on the ceremony programs.

- ☐ Have your bachelorette party.

- ☐ Buy your wedding veil and all accessories (in time for your final fitting).

- ☐ Decide on your something old, new, borrowed, and blue.

- ☐ Make a plan for kids at your reception and arrange a babysitter, if necessary.

- ☐ Research local marriage license requirements.

- ☐ Confirm out-of-town-guest hotel reservations and check with the hotel to make sure you don't need to block out more rooms.

- ☐ Have your first dress fitting.

- ☐ Schedule hair and makeup trial appointments to take place 3–4 weeks ahead of time.

- ☐ Get going on thank-you notes for those gifts received already.

1 month before   by ___ /___

- ☐ Finalize the ceremony. Schedule a follow-up meeting with your officiant to go over timing and details.

- ☐ Finish your ceremony programs.

- ☐ Send out rehearsal dinner invites (if you didn't include them in the invites).

- ☐ Work out a day-of schedule to time out all of the details (hour by hour).

- ☐ Plan any night-before activities with friends and/or attendants.

- ☐ Purchase gifts for parents and each other.

- ☐ Purchase gifts for attendants.

- ☐ Plan, order, or shop for welcome bags for out-of-town guests.

1–2 weeks before

- ☐ Call guests who have not yet returned their reply cards.

- ☐ Put the seating chart together and give copies to your caterer, reception site manager, and planner. (See page 198.)

- ☐ Give your caterer, cake baker, and reception site manager the final head count. Include vendors, such as band members and the photographer, who will expect a meal. (Also, ask how many extra plates the caterer will prepare—that is, the full plate count.)

- ☐ Supply the reception site manager with a list of requests from other vendors (such as a table for the DJ, setup space needed by the florist, and so on).

- ☐ Work on escort cards and their display.

- ☐ Confirm transportation for the day.
- ☐ Shop and pack for the honeymoon.
- ☐ Confirm all final payment amounts, details, and delivery and location times with your vendors (florist, cake baker, photographer, DJ/band).
- ☐ Distribute a key contacts list including the bride, groom, wedding party members, planner, and key vendors.
- ☐ Confirm and distribute the day-of schedule to all parents, attendants, and vendors.
- ☐ Prepare your wedding toasts and/or thanks to friends and family.
- ☐ Practice walking in your wedding shoes.
- ☐ Have your final dress fitting.
- ☐ Put together an overnight bag for the wedding night.
- ☐ Confirm your honeymoon itinerary; give a copy to your parents.
- ☐ Put final payments and gratuities in labeled envelopes for distribution on the wedding day.
- ☐ Compile a must-take photo list for the photographer, including who should be in formal portraits.
- ☐ Apply for a marriage license together in the town where you'll wed (you may need to go three weeks before).
- ☐ Deliver to your DJ or bandleader a list of special song requests and any songs you definitely want or don't want played.
- ☐ Get one last prewedding haircut or trim and hair color touch-up.
- ☐ Arrange airport pickups for key family members who can't or won't be renting a car.

2–3 days before

- ☐ Arrange and confirm transportation to the airport for your honeymoon.
- ☐ Organize your day-of emergency kit.
- ☐ Have your dress pressed or steamed, if you still need to.
- ☐ Wrap gifts for parents, attendants, and each other. Write notes.
- ☐ Touch base with the ceremony and reception venues one more time.
- ☐ In preparation for the rehearsal, determine the order of bridesmaids and groomsmen in the processional and recessional.
- ☐ If the caterer will be arranging place cards, table cards, menu cards, and/or the guest book, hand them off.
- ☐ Reconfirm that the florist received your (correct) flower order and knows where and when the flowers should be delivered. Should the personal flowers go to the ceremony site or to your home or hotel?
- ☐ Confirm all locations and pickup times with the limousine company or driver.
- ☐ Deliver welcome bags to out-of-town guests' hotel rooms (get attendants to help).
- ☐ Confirm all toasts with your wedding party, friends, and family.

day before

- ☐ Get your manicure and/or pedicure.

- ☐ Bring the unity candle, aisle runner, yarmulke, or other ceremony accessories to the site so you won't have to think about them on the wedding morning.

- ☐ Rehearse the ceremony.

- ☐ Give your marriage license to your officiant.

- ☐ Have fun (but not too much fun) at your rehearsal dinner or welcome party.

- ☐ Give attendants their gifts at the rehearsal dinner (especially if they're accessories to be worn during the wedding).

- ☐ Prepare the hair and makeup schedule for the bridesmaids and make them promise to live by it.

- ☐ Get a good night's sleep!

day of

- ☐ Shoot to get your hair and makeup session done early so you aren't stressed out.

- ☐ Present parents (and each other) with gifts or at least a big hug and kiss.

- ☐ Give the best man and/or maid of honor your wedding rings.

- ☐ Give your father or the best man the officiant's fee envelope, to be handed off after the ceremony.

- ☐ Introduce your reception manager and consultant or maid of honor (if that hasn't happened already) so they can deal with any questions or problems during the party.

- ☐ Have fun and enjoy your day!

postwedding

- ☐ Make a note of any stains on your dress and send it off for a proper cleaning and preservation.

- ☐ Return formalwear rentals.

- ☐ Freeze the top layer of your cake.

- ☐ If preserving your bouquet, send it to a preservation service.

- ☐ Send each of your vendors a thank-you note.

- ☐ Write online reviews of your venue, photographer, etc., so that future brides know what to expect!

- ☐ When you return from your honeymoon, call and thank each of your attendants one more time.

- ☐ Keep a gift log (see appendix) and send out those thank-you notes as soon as possible.

express engagement checklist

(5 MONTHS OR LESS)

If you have five months or less, dive in and make those big decisions as soon as possible. Prioritize—don't get tied up in all the details. If you have an even shorter engagement, truncate this list even further to make it work within your schedule.

4–5 months before   by ___ /___

☐ Tackle the following: wedding date and time, wedding budget, and initial guest list.

☐ Interview and book a wedding planner.

☐ Book your photographer.

☐ Book your videographer.

☐ Book an officiant.

☐ Book your ceremony and reception locations.

☐ Book your caterer.

☐ Book your florist.

☐ Book your reception band or DJ.

☐ Choose your bridal party.

☐ Choose your wedding dress (you might need to go off-the-rack or buy a sample).

☐ Decide on bridesmaid dresses (probably off-the-rack or at a national chain online).

☐ Decide on groom and groomsmen formalwear.

☐ Buy bridesmaid dresses (probably off-the-rack).

☐ Order flower girl and ring bearer attire.

☐ Create your wedding website. (Check out TheKnot.com/pwp.) Then update with venue and hotel info as you plan.

☐ Compile the final guest list with all addresses (keep track of it at TheKnot.com/guestlist).

☐ Send save-the-date cards (if there's no time and a guest list of less than 50, consider e-mailing them).

☐ Decide whether you need any other vendors (lighting, rental companies).

☐ Reserve a block of rooms for out-of-town guests.

☐ Get your engagement ring appraised and insured.

☐ Order invitations, thank-you notes, and any other wedding day stationery you plan to send.

3 months before   by ___ /___

☐ Set up your registry.

☐ Book your rehearsal dinner space.

☐ Hire ceremony musicians.

☐ Choose a cake baker.

☐ Book transportation.

☐ Order veil and any other accessories.

☐ Research honeymoon spots.

☐ Reach out to out-of-town guests and let them know about your wedding website.

☐ Shop for wedding rings.

☐ Have those engagement photos taken.

☐ Put together guest lists for showers.

☐ Plan the ceremony with your officiant.

☐ Make dress-fitting appointments.

☐ Order rehearsal dinner invites.

timeline & budget

2 months before   by ____ / ____

- ☐ Send out invitations (6–8 weeks beforehand).
- ☐ Choose your menu and have a tasting.
- ☐ Book the honeymoon.
- ☐ Hire a hair and makeup artist.
- ☐ Buy wedding party gifts.
- ☐ Research marriage license requirements.
- ☐ Buy any extras you'll need to wear under your dress.
- ☐ Figure out your floral proposal with your florist, and finalize décor and bouquets.
- ☐ Make DJ/band a list of must-plays and do-not-plays.
- ☐ Have your first fitting.

5–7 weeks before   by ____ / ____

- ☐ Sign up for professional dance lessons.
- ☐ Decide on favors.
- ☐ Get welcome gifts for out-of-towners.
- ☐ Have your final meeting with your reception musicians or DJ.
- ☐ Mail out those rehearsal dinner invites.

3–4 weeks before   by ____ / ____

- ☐ Work on your ceremony vows.
- ☐ Start working on the ceremony programs.
- ☐ Buy your wedding veil, shoes, and all accessories (in time for your final fitting). Decide on your "something old, new, borrowed, and blue."
- ☐ Make a kids' plan for the reception.
- ☐ Confirm out-of-town guests' hotel reservations.
- ☐ Schedule hair and makeup trial appointments.

- ☐ Get going on thank-you notes for those gifts received already.
- ☐ Finalize the ceremony. Schedule a follow-up meeting with your officiant to go over timing and details.
- ☐ Finish your ceremony programs.
- ☐ Send out rehearsal dinner invites.
- ☐ Work out a day-of schedule.
- ☐ Plan any night-before activities.
- ☐ Purchase gifts for parents, attendants, and each other.

1–2 weeks before   by ____ / ____

- ☐ Call guests who have not yet returned their invitation response cards.
- ☐ Put the seating chart together and give it to your caterer, manager, and planner.
- ☐ Give your caterer, cake baker, and reception site manager the final head count. Include vendors, such as band members and the photographer, who will expect a meal. (Also, ask how many extra plates the caterer will prepare; that is, the plate count.)
- ☐ Supply the reception site manager with a list of requests from other vendors (such as a table for the DJ, setup space needed by the florist, and so on).
- ☐ Work on escort cards and seating chart.
- ☐ Confirm transportation for the day.
- ☐ Shop and pack for the honeymoon.
- ☐ Confirm all final payment amounts, details, and delivery and location times with your vendors. Also, compile their phone numbers to distribute.
- ☐ Confirm and distribute the day-of schedule and contact list to all parents, attendants, and vendors.

- ☐ Prepare your wedding toasts.

- ☐ Practice walking in your wedding shoes.

- ☐ Have your final dress fitting.

- ☐ Put together an overnight bag for the wedding night.

- ☐ Leave a copy of your honeymoon itinerary with close friends and family.

- ☐ Put final payments and cash tips for vendors in envelopes, and give to a friend to distribute on the wedding day.

- ☐ Compile a must-take photo list for the photographer.

- ☐ Apply for a marriage license together (you may need to go 3 weeks before).

- ☐ Draw up and deliver to your DJ or bandleader a list of special song requests.

- ☐ If needed, give your videographer a must-shoot list.

- ☐ Get one last haircut or trim and hair-color touch-up.

- ☐ Arrange for guests who will not rent cars to be picked up from the airport or train station.

2 or 3 days before

- ☐ Arrange and confirm transportation to the airport for your honeymoon.

- ☐ Organize your day-of emergency kit.

- ☐ If your dress still needs to be pressed or steamed, do this now.

- ☐ Wrap gifts for parents, attendants, and each other. Write notes.

- ☐ Touch base with the ceremony and reception venues one more time.

- ☐ In preparation for the rehearsal, determine the order of bridesmaids and groomsmen in the processional and recessional.

- ☐ If the caterer will be arranging place cards, table cards, menu cards, and/or the guest book, hand them off.

- ☐ Reconfirm that the florist received your (correct) flower order and knows where and when the flowers should be delivered. Should the personal flowers go to the ceremony site or to your home or hotel?

- ☐ Confirm all locations and pickup times with the limousine company or driver.

- ☐ Deliver welcome baskets to out-of-town guests' hotel rooms (get attendants to help).

- ☐ Confirm all toasts with your wedding party, friends, and family.

day before

- ☐ Get your manicure and/or pedicure.

- ☐ Bring the unity candle, aisle runner, yarmulke, or other ceremony accessories to the site so you won't have to think about them on the wedding morning.

- ☐ Rehearse the ceremony.

- ☐ Give your marriage license to your officiant.

- ☐ Have fun (but not too much fun) at your rehearsal dinner or welcome party.

- ☐ Give attendants their gifts at the rehearsal dinner (especially if they're accessories to be worn during the wedding).

- ☐ Prepare the hair and makeup schedule for the bridesmaids and make them promise to live by it.

- ☐ Get a good night's sleep!

day of

- ☐ Shoot to get to your hair and makeup session done early so you aren't stressed out.

- ☐ Present parents (and each other) with gifts or at least a big hug and kiss.

- ☐ Give the best man and/or maid of honor your wedding rings.

- ☐ Give your father or the best man the officiant's fee envelope, to be handed off after the ceremony.

- ☐ Introduce your reception manager and consultant or maid of honor (if that hasn't happened already) so they can deal with any questions or problems during the party.

- ☐ Have fun and enjoy your day!

postwedding

- ☐ Make a note of any stains on your dress and send it off for a proper cleaning and preservation.

- ☐ Return formalwear rentals.

- ☐ Freeze the top layer of your cake.

- ☐ If preserving your bouquet, send it to a preservation service.

- ☐ Send each of your vendors a thank-you note.

- ☐ Write online reviews of your venue, photographer, etc., so that future brides know what to expect!

- ☐ When you return from your honeymoon, call and thank each of your attendants one more time.

- ☐ Keep a gift log (see appendix) and send out those thank-you notes as soon as possible.

top planning tips

1 make a statement
Be creative. Use your relationship history, heritage, or favorite colors or activities as inspiration for a more personal party.

2 pick your battles
Don't obsess over every single detail. Sit down and decide your top priorities and then spend most of your budget, energy, and attention on those items.

3 study up
Weddings have their very own lingo.

4 ask lots of questions
Don't ever be afraid that your questions are too stupid. Don't hire anyone until you've got a good answer to every question here.

5 trust yourself
Know the proper etiquette, but decide whether to apply every rule to the situation.

6 get it in writing
You're spending a lot of money. Protect yourself by making sure all details are down on paper and signed by both parties. Contract points for each vendor are delineated in each chapter; check off everything on the list before you sign. Every time you make any kind of payment, do the following: (1) If no invoice is provided, draw up a letter noting the date, the payment amount, exactly what the payment is supposed to cover, the check number, and so on. Keep a copy for yourself. (2) Make a copy of every check you write and get credit card receipts. Staple these to your invoice or letter and keep them in your folder.

7 use a credit card
If the terms of the contract you draw up with a professional are not met, you can call your credit card company and dispute payment. If you pay in cash, you don't have any recourse. There's no need to inherently distrust your wedding professionals, of course, but you'll want to protect your investment, as you would with any other big-ticket item. Be aware that some professionals won't take credit cards; ask when you agree to work together. Make sure the credit card you do use accumulates frequent-flier miles—they may just cover your honeymoon flight.

8 read reviews and check references
Never sign a contract with a vendor before you call past clients and check their online wedding reviews (TheKnot.com/reviews). Make sure you have recent references—from the past year. Ask references detailed questions, such as: Were there any charges on your final bill that you did not expect? Was there anything that you wish the vendor would've done differently? Did the courses served (or flowers used, or songs played) reflect what you had decided on?

9 have a life outside of wedding planning
A crash diet consisting only of wedding planning can kill the mood. Declare wedding-free zones with each other where all talk of table cards and canapés is completely forbidden.

(CONTINUES)

10 consider a planner

Hire a wedding planner if (1) neither you nor your families (read: moms) have time to plan your wedding; (2) neither you nor your families have any desire to plan your wedding; (3) you're planning a wedding out of town; or (4) you simply prefer—and can afford—professional help. They'll do the legwork, hire vendors, and negotiate your contracts, and may even save you some money. Expect to pay 10 to 15 percent of your total wedding budget. Search TheKnot.com/planners for listings by city and read page 19 on hiring a wedding planner.

ASK CARLEY

wedding planning etiquette

How long should our engagement be?

There is no right engagement length. Some people get married in three months, some in three years. The longer you have before your wedding date, the better the chance that you'll get the best vendors. Start nailing down your date, sites, and, most important, vendors ASAP. Another great reason for a long engagement is to save up wedding funds. (See the worksheet on page 35.) If your wedding is years off, keep in mind that some places may not take reservations until two years in advance. If it's mere months until your desired date, don't hesitate to call around and see what and who is available; last-minute cancellations do happen.

Who throws the engagement party? Is it okay to invite people who won't be invited to the wedding?

It's the bride's family's prerogative to throw the first engagement party; after they have done so (or determined not to), the groom's family gets a turn. Some couples plan their own laid-back bash with friends and close relatives at a favorite bar or restaurant. Gifts are optional, but because many guests do choose to give them, you'll want to register beforehand. If you don't intend to invite them to the wedding, don't invite them to the engagement party.

your wedding budget

Don't spend one dollar until you've figured out your wedding budget. Call or sit down with anyone who might be contributing, and politely find out how much they're willing to commit. Do the calculations and get yourself some guidelines.

your budget estimates

Before you can begin talking to any vendors, you need to know approximately how much you have to spend in each category. Here are some averages to help you get started. Use the budget worksheet in the appendix to track your actual expenses through the process.

your budget

Your priorities may be different, so feel free to move percentages and money around accordingly.

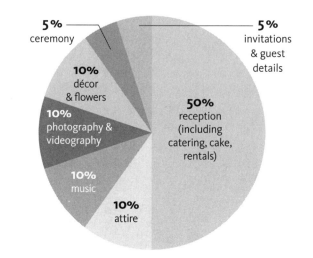

5%
ceremony

5%
invitations & guest details

10%
décor & flowers

10%
photography & videography

50%
reception (including catering, cake, rentals)

10%
music

10%
attire

TIPS
other fees to watch for

taxes
You're always going to have to add tax to the total. Make sure it's accounted for.

delivery, setup & breakdown costs
Get this factored into your contracts so that it doesn't come as a surprise.

service charges & standard tips
Most venues tack on a service charge and tips (for their waitstaff).

overtime
You'll pay dearly for going over at the reception. Check your contracts for this.

the knot TIP
Track all your expenses online (and set up reminders for yourself) at **TheKnot.com/budgeter.**

wedding budget worksheet

your contribution

$ _____ x _____ = $ _____
your savings   % of savings you're   your existing wedding
            willing to contribute   contribution

your savings potential

$ _____ x _____ + _____ = $ _____
your combined   # of months   % of income you   your potential wedding
monthly income   engaged   plan to contribute   contribution

bride's parents' contribution (if applicable) $ _____

groom's parents' contribution (if applicable) $ _____

anyone else's contribution (if applicable) $ _____

total wedding budget $ _____

your estimated wedding budget breakdown

category	%	example	your estimates
		($30,000)	
Reception site, rentals, food, drink, cake	x .50	$15,000	$ _____
Wedding dress and formalwear	x .10	$3,000	$ _____
Flowers and décor	x .10	$3,000	$ _____
Photo and video	x .10	$3,000	$ _____
Music	x .10	$3,000	$ _____
Invitations and guest details	x .05	$1,500	$ _____
Ceremony site and officiant	x .05	$1,500	$ _____

When you get a price quote from a vendor, don't forget to factor in taxes and tips.

NOTE: The following big-ticket items are not included: honeymoon (can run upward of $3,000); wedding consultant (up to 15 percent of total budget); rehearsal dinner.

top wedding budget tips

Think you can't have the wedding you want with your budget? No matter how big, a budget is still a budget. Here's how to make your wedding fund go even further.

1 **cut down**
Invite a hundred guests instead of a hundred and fifty; serve three courses instead of five; have two bridesmaids instead of ten.

2 **be flexible**
Offer a limited bar of beer, wine, and soft drinks rather than the pricier full bar.

3 **pick and choose**
Indulge in a designer dress, but don't go all out on your getaway car; serve a great cake and skip the dessert table.

4 **put it off**
Get silver wedding bands and upgrade to platinum on your first anniversary; exchange gifts at the six-month mark; take a honeymoon close to home and then go someplace far-flung later.

5 **do it yourself**
Make your own ceremony programs or wedding favors and address your own envelopes. Save the bigger details (flowers, music, cake, photos) for the pros, though.

6 **consider a night other than saturday**
There will probably be better availability for Friday and Sunday (or even Thursday) dates, and you may be able to get a lower rate on the space.

7 **stay in season**
You'll save big on flowers.

8 **opt for local ingredients**
You'll save on importing costs.

9 **repurpose flowers**
Take ceremony flowers along to the reception site. Or arrange to share the cost of ceremony decorations with the couple marrying directly before or after you that day.

10 **during cocktail hour, instead of an open bar, serve wine in passed glasses**
Or serve a signature cocktail that uses less, or less expensive, liquor.

11 **if your caterer and reception site allow, buy the alcohol yourselves**
You may be able to return unopened cases, instead of paying your caterer or banquet manager a flat rate for a set amount of open-bar hours.

12 **ask stationers whether a discounted package price is available** if you order all your stationery at once (announcements, invitations, thank-yous).

4

your guest list

How many people to invite (and exactly whom) is one of the biggest decisions you need to make during this initial sketching period. This may sound like one of the most pleasurable aspects of your wedding preparation—the two of you sitting down over a bottle of wine, taking stock of all the wonderful people you'll share this special day with. But the truth is, making the guest list is difficult, given all the forces (parental opinions, budgetary concerns, reception site considerations) pulling you in different directions.

wedding guest worksheet

Once you have a sense of your venue size, it's time to decide who's in and who's out. Traditionally, the bride and her family and the groom and his folks each invite half of the guests, with the parents on both sides—usually the major check writers—calling most of the shots. But if you and your fiancé are underwriting the majority of the reception costs, it's acceptable for you to determine the bulk of the guest list. Another arrangement that works well is to divide the rations three ways: between the soon-to-be-weds, the bride's parents, and the groom's parents. If your parents are divorced, you're going to have to make more divisions.

Total guest list   # _____

who gets to invite and how many guests?

You (the couple)   # _____   Groom's parents   # _____
Bride's parents   # _____   Other   # _____

Once you've drafted your initial list, export it to TheKnot.com/guestlist to track it all online.

your personal wedding website

Everything from hotel room blocks to transportation info and pertinent times should go on your wedding website. (Create yours at **TheKnot.com/websites.**)

a few essentials for your wedding website

☐ How you met/got engaged, plus any photos

☐ Links to your registries

☐ Details on ceremony and reception sites and times

☐ Details on hotel accommodations and transportation

☐ Any other activities you have planned

☐ A guest book (for guests to share their warm wishes!)

not necessary (but very fun) ideas for your wedding website

☐ Polling (like where you should go on your honeymoon)

☐ Guest-of-the-week spotlights (your favorite aunt, your grandma)

☐ Videos (from the day he proposed, your engagement party)

top guest list tips

1 create two lists

Start by creating your fantasy list—all the friends and family you'd like to have at your wedding. Then split the list into two groups: friends and family that you absolutely have to have, and the rest of the invitees in order of importance. It sounds harsh, but it's the best way to keep them organized.

2 create criteria for cutting

At some point, you'll more than likely be faced with trimming the guest list. Make it easier on yourselves by setting up some rules. For example, maybe you cut any kids under age 10; decide not to extend an "and guest" to single friends unless they're in a serious relationship; cut all coworkers; or limit the list to only first cousins in both families.

3 mind the budget

More guests on the list means more money spent on the food and venue. There are ways to cut costs, but a bigger list will mean you'll have to work with a smaller budget in other places (like flowers and décor).

4 establish quotas early

Ideally, you should be able to divide the guest list equally between you and your families. Then again, money talks. If your parents are footing part or all of the bill, you're going to have to hear them out when they suggest inviting their coworkers and close friends. Your mantra here: compromise.

5 curb the guilt

A wedding isn't the time to round up every long-lost friend you've known since childhood. Don't feel bad when you run into people you haven't seen in years and aren't planning on inviting them to the wedding even if they invited you to theirs.

6 don't be pushed by parents

Set and stick to boundaries. This can be tricky if one set of parents is paying and demands a greater slice of the guest list. But this is your event. Sometimes it's just a matter of increasing the guest-list size, and the parent who goes over his or her number of invites can finance the overflow. But often your site caps the guest count. If that's the case, be resolute.

7 save-the-dates

An early save-the-date via e-mail is a great way to collect addresses. Just be sure everyone on your save-the-date list will actually be invited to the wedding.

guest list etiquette

We're having a small wedding. Do we have to include "and guest" on single people's invitations? If we don't, what if someone replies for two anyway?

Most guests understand that without "and guest" or another name on the invitation, it's meant for them alone. If you're having a small wedding, you probably aren't going to be able to invite everyone with a date, unless it's a fiancé and/or a serious significant other. (Technically, you're never supposed to use "and guest." Instead, you should find out the name of the date, but you've probably seen "and guest" a lot anyway, because it's easier than asking everyone whom they're planning to bring.) What to do if a clueless soul replies for two? Call and explain that you're having an intimate wedding and were not able to invite everyone with a guest, but that you will call that person immediately if a space opens up.

Are out-of-towners supposed to be invited to the rehearsal dinner?

You don't have to invite them. A rehearsal dinner can be as simple as your immediate families and wedding party, plus their spouses or significant others. It's a very good opportunity to spend some time with visiting friends and relatives—you'll be more relaxed than at the wedding, and you'll probably be able to chat with people you might not get a chance to really sit down with later. If you want to maximize your quality time with those out-of-towners, invite them. If you decide not to, don't leave them hanging—be sure some sort of party or event is planned for them, or that they have some ideas for how to entertain themselves.

Can I invite guests to the ceremony but not the reception?

Avoid this if at all possible. People may feel bad if you invite them to the wedding but then don't include them in the celebration afterward; they may even suspect you did it only to get a gift! The one exception: If you are active in your church or temple, you may want to extend an open invitation to the ceremony to the entire congregation.

What about inviting guests to the reception but not the ceremony?

It's okay to do this if you have your heart set on a super-intimate, family-only vow exchange but want to party with all your friends and loved ones afterward.

If we're asking guests to travel and stay overnight, do we have to pay their way?

You're not responsible for your guests' airfare or overnight costs, and most people are well aware of this fact. What you can do is recommend places for them to stay. Many hotels offer a discounted group rate if you book a certain number of rooms for your wedding. If certain guests can't afford to stay in a hotel, try to arrange for them to stay with local bridesmaids, groomsmen, relatives, or friends (preferably people they already know). Don't invite out-of-towners to stay with you (unless it's your maid of honor we're talking about). You'll have enough stress already!

invitations

The invitations are your guests' first impression of your wedding, so make sure they reflect the spirit, style, and formality of the celebration. Spend some time familiarizing yourself with all the specific wording conventions and addressing rules—if only to understand what others will expect. In order to send invitations out at the three-month mark, you'll want to start your search four or five months out. If you're concerned about scheduling conflicts, send a save-the-date card as soon as you nail down your wedding date.

invitations style worksheet

Wedding invitations give guests a sneak peek at what's to come. Every choice you make—from color to paper, printing, and even wording—will act as your style translator.

style

☐ Formal   ☐ Classic   ☐ Floral   ☐ Understated

☐ Ornate   ☐ Graphic   ☐ Creative   ☐ Casual

☐ Themed   ☐ Colorful   ☐ Botanical   ☐ Vintage

lettering

☐ *script*   ☐ serif   ☐ slab serif

☐ sans serif   ☐ *copperplate*

printing style

☐ Engraving   ☐ Thermography   ☐ Letterpress   ☐ Calligraphy

names and information to be listed on invitation (Decide exactly how your names will be written out. Typically, you'll want to go more formal, as in "Rebecca" instead of "Becky.")

☐ Bride _____

☐ Groom _____

☐ Bride's parents, stepparents _____

_____

☐ Groom's parents, stepparents _____

_____

☐ Wedding date and time _____

☐ Ceremony site name and address _____

_____

☐ Reception site name and address _____

_____

invitations needed #_____
(**NOTE:** The number is not going to be equal to the guest-list size; each couple/family will get only one invitation.)

invitation and stationery budget $_____

top invite planning tips

1 look around

Mixing type styles is an innovative way to change up your invitation's look. Flip through design books and magazines for inspiration. By checking out what's hot in graphic design, you're sure to find a cutting-edge look.

2 know how to save

Keep it simple. Top-quality paper and custom artwork will raise the price, and so will decorative envelope linings and multiple enclosures. Use response postcards instead of cards, or have guests RSVP online (use the service at TheKnot.com/rsvp). If you're concerned about postage, stay away from oversize or overweight styles. Avoid engraving and letterpress.

3 overorder

Don't order the exact number of invites you'll need—get at least twenty extra. It's better to have leftovers than to have to reorder later. Also order extra envelopes to leave room for addressing errors. (If you're hiring a calligrapher, she may ask for a certain percentage of extras.) You'll send one invitation per household (not per guest), but a child over eighteen living at home gets his own invite.

4 double-check everything

Make sure you check your proof very precisely for spelling, dates, and times. (Double-check the calendar!) Have a smart, grammar-inclined friend or two look it over too. Any last-minute changes after the proof will cost you.

5 handwrite the envelopes

It's customary to handwrite your guests' addresses instead of typing or printing out labels.

6 get a head start

When you order your invitations, see if you can take the envelopes home immediately—or, if you're having a return address printed on them, at least request that they be delivered ASAP—so you can start addressing them (or have a calligrapher do so) while the invites are at the printer.

7 keep it neat

Ask the post office to hand-cancel each one of your delicately crafted invites (instead of running it through the machine) to keep it in tip-top shape. Running them through a stamping machine may cause smears or crinkle your design.

8 add your website

Keep guests up-to-date (and avoid the hassle of having to include every last bit of information in print) by including your website URL on your invitation. Put it at the bottom of the invite or include a separate card (a more formal option).

9 don't change it up (yet)

Don't forget—you're not married yet! Save your new monogram for the thank-you cards, and opt for your initials (full initials or intertwining first letters, for example) for the invites.

10 say thanks!

The thank-you-note project begins way back when you gather your guests' names and addresses to send the invitations. Do yourself a big favor: Save that list! When you start opening presents, record each gift next to the giver's name and address.

guest list, invitations & wedding party

finding your stationer

To find a stationery provider, consider both large stationery stores and small independent invitation designers. Ordering your invitations online is also a simple (and often cost-effective) option. Browse hundreds of options at **TheKnot.com/invitations,** and make appointments with several stationery designers.

designer/store name _____	designer/store name _____
website _____	website _____
e-mail _____	e-mail _____
address _____	address _____
phone _____	phone _____
referred by _____	referred by _____
app't date ___ /___ /___ time _____	app't date ___ /___ /___ time _____
price estimate $ _____	price estimate $ _____

ASK CARLEY
invitations & stationery etiquette

How do I assemble my invitations?

Depending on the style you've chosen, you'll leave them flat or fold them in half or in fourths. The text should be on the front, the fold on the left. Tuck enclosure cards inside, or set them on top of the larger card. Put the pile in an ungummed inner envelope, with the print visible upon opening the flap. Leave the inner envelope unsealed. Once you've written the guests' names on the inner envelope, place it inside the outer envelope, with the names facing the flap. Address the outer envelope, seal, and stamp; you're done!

questions to ask
stationery designers

Does he design custom invitations or sell invitation lines? If the latter, how many lines does he carry?

_____

_____

Is there a style or type of invitation she specializes in (traditional styles, theme invitations)?

_____

_____

Are there sample books to browse through? (This will give you a great idea of whether the stationer's work matches with what you want.)

_____

_____

What about calligraphy? (If there's no in-house calligrapher, he may be able to refer you.)

_____

_____

Does she have a sample wording guide?

_____

_____

Once he places your order, will you be able to see a proof (what the invitation will look like) before the actual invitations are ready? What happens if there's an error on the order?

_____

_____

How long after you place an order will your invitations come in?

_____

_____

Are you allowed to do your own creative wording? Confirm that she will not change the wording to reflect her understanding of the rules of etiquette.

_____

_____

How are invitations priced? Is there any benefit to purchasing other wedding stationery at the same time? Is there any form of price list?

_____

_____

Does he sell other personalized items (coordinating save-the-dates, welcome bags, favor tags)?

_____

_____

stationer contact cheat sheet

stationery designers/store _____

contact/point person _____

website _____

phone _____

e-mail _____

address _____

_____

number and type of invitations ordered

_____

other stationery ordered

estimate $ _____

deposit $ _____ date paid _____

total cost $ _____

balance $ _____ date due _____

calligraphy cost $ _____

notes _____

_____

_____

_____

ASK CARLEY
invitations & stationery etiquette

What are the guidelines for inner-envelope addressing?

The formal way is with titles only: "Mr. and Mrs. Smith"; "Ms. Adams and Mr. Zorn" (alphabetically, if a couple has different last names); "Dr. and Mrs. Jones" (if you need to use a professional title). If your wedding is more casual and intimate, you can just use first names or familiar titles (Aunt Emma).

What about the outer envelope?

Guests' names and mailing addresses should be written out in full on the outer envelope—Mr. and Mrs. Paul Daly, Ms. Jacqueline Underberg, and so on. Always spell out the words *Street, Lane,* and *Apartment.* Your stationer will probably have a booklet all about titles and addressing that will help you with other specific questions you have. You can also find all these details at TheKnot.com/invitations.

ordering your invites & stationery

☐ Based on the styles and services available, choose your stationer.

☐ Type out exact invitation wording and get okays from all involved.

☐ Finalize invitation choices
  ☐ Design/designer _____
  ☐ Paper/weight _____
  ☐ Ink color(s) _____
  ☐ Font(s) _____
  ☐ Style of printing _____

☐ Determine list of all stationery elements needed

invitations

☐ Outer envelopes (mailing envelopes, addressed with full names and addresses) # _____

☐ Inner envelopes (optional unsealed packaging envelopes for all materials) # _____

☐ Reply envelopes (self-addressed, stamped envelopes for RSVPs) # _____

☐ Invitations # _____

☐ Reception cards (optional cards listing information for the reception) # _____

☐ Response cards # _____

extras

☐ Save-the-date cards (send 6–8 months in advance so guests can make travel arrangements early, if needed) # _____

☐ Travel information (printed maps, directions, or location information may be sent with the save-the-dates or the invitation) # _____

☐ Accommodation information # _____

☐ Morning-after brunch # _____

☐ Rehearsal dinner invite # _____

☐ Pew cards # _____

☐ In-case-of-rain cards # _____

☐ Thank-you notes and envelopes # _____

☐ Wedding announcements # _____

wedding day stationery

☐ Ceremony programs # _____

☐ Signage for the ceremony or reception # _____

☐ Menu cards # _____

☐ Escort cards # _____

☐ Place cards # _____

☐ Favor labels # _____

☐ Napkins (stamped with your logo) # _____

☐ Welcome-bag tags # _____

☐ Place your order. Review contract or receipt for the following critical points:

  ☐ Name and contact information for you and the vendor

  ☐ The exact wording of your invitation and all enclosures, printed, with correct line breaks

  ☐ The return address to be printed on the envelopes

  ☐ The mailing address to be printed on RSVPs

  ☐ Paper stock and color

  ☐ Ink color

  ☐ Typeface to be used (a sample should be attached)

  ☐ Printing style (thermography, engraving)

  ☐ Descriptions and amounts of other stationery and accessories ordered

(CONTINUES)

guest list, invitations & wedding party

☐ Date the order will be ready

☐ Total price

☐ Deposit amount due

☐ Balance and date due

☐ Cancellation and refund policy

☐ Stationer's signature

☐ Proofread the order to make sure all information is factually correct and there are no typos. (Triple-check all addresses.)

☐ Type website URL into browser to confirm.

☐ Sign contract or receipt.

☐ Have the store send you a proof before the print job is run; proofread carefully and fix any errors.

☐ Hire a calligrapher to address your envelopes.

☐ When your order comes in, count invitations and envelopes and proofread.

☐ If you haven't yet, buy thank-you notes.

☐ Take a finished invitation to the post office to weigh for proper postage.

☐ Choose your stamps, or order custom stamps.

☐ Mail your invitations three months before the wedding. Ask the post office to hand-cancel your invites.

how to word your invites

Hosts (choose one and fill in the blank)

☐ If one set of parents is hosting:
Mr. and Mrs. _____

☐ If both sets of parents are hosting:
Mr. and Mrs. _____
and
Mr. and Mrs. _____

☐ If you two are hosting:
Ms. _____
and
Mr. _____

☐ If a divorced parent is hosting:
Ms./Mrs./Mr. _____

Request line (choose one):

☐ Request the pleasure of your company

☐ Request the honor of your presence

☐ At their marriage (if you two are hosting)

☐ At the marriage of their children (if both your parents are hosting)

☐ At the marriage of their/his/her daughter (if one set of parents is hosting)

☐ Couple's names if they aren't hosting (fill in the blank):
Your name _____
and
Fiancé's name _____

Date and time (fill in the blanks):

On _____ (day), the _____ (date)
of _____ (month)

Two thousand and _____

At _____ (hour) o'clock in the _____
(morning, afternoon, or evening)

Location (fill in the blank) _____

_____

_____
(ceremony venue, city, and state)

your wedding party

6

You can have just honor attendants or you can have teams of seven on each side. Guys can be bridesmaids, and a dog can do the duties of the ring bearer. To avoid hurt feelings, make it clear early what style of involvement by family and friends you want. Also, never assume all members know what they're supposed to do when you assign them their title. Be clear about their duties.

your wedding party worksheet

ceremony roles

Which of the following (and how many of each) would you like to have? Jot down names where obvious.

☐ Maid/matron of honor _____

☐ Bridesmaids (#_____)

_____   _____

_____   _____

_____   _____

☐ Best man _____   _____

☐ Groomsmen (#_____)

_____   _____

_____   _____

_____   _____

☐ Ushers (#_____)

_____   _____

_____   _____

☐ Ring bearer(s) _____

☐ Flower girl(s) _____

☐ Reader(s)/performer(s) _____

_____

☐ Other (assistants needed for holding the huppah, handing out programs or scattering flower petals, lighting candles, helping perform other religious or ethnic rituals, and so on)

_____

_____

_____

_____

top wedding party tips

1 think before you ask

It's easy to get caught up in all the excitement, but before you ask your favorite coworker to be your bridesmaid, take a step back and consider who will be there for you not just during the planning process, but also five and ten years from now. In other words, fill that spot with his sister (your future sister-in-law).

2 skip the symmetry

You don't need the same number of attendants on each side; if the bride wants five maids and the groom has only three, that's fine.

3 kids are optional

If there are no children you two feel particularly close to, you don't need a flower girl or ring bearer. And if you have many children you want to include, feel free. Give them the role of pages or flower children.

4 how "special" is that role, really?

If you're feeling bad about not being able to include someone as an attendant, think twice before offering them a position such as "guest-book watcher." Would you want to do that? They'll be happier with a VIP corsage and a reserved seat at the ceremony.

5 don't want a wedding party?

You don't need attendants. We know plenty of couples who have done away with the idea of a traditional wedding party and found other ways to make their favorite friends and family feel special.

ASK CARLEY
wedding party

Ever since we got engaged, my mom has turned into a bit of a control freak. How do I deal?

Weddings are a huge deal for parents so it's important to listen to your parents' desires and priorities, and even if you don't completely agree, give a little in places that are important to them. A few tips to get mom involved: ask her opinion instead of trying to dodge it; put her in charge of duties she's interested in and excited about but that you don't feel the need to control; and be sure to thank her with a gift of gratitude, be it a spa gift certificate or a framed photo of you two.

guest list, invitations & wedding party

honor attendant cheat sheet

maid of honor

I want my maid of honor to . . .

PREWEDDING

- ☐ Y ☐ N Help bride shop for gown
- ☐ Y ☐ N Help bride shop for bridesmaid dresses
- ☐ Y ☐ N Spread word about couple's registry
- ☐ Y ☐ N Coordinate bridesmaids' dress orders, payment, and fittings
- ☐ Y ☐ N Plan shower and/or bachelorette party
- ☐ Y ☐ N Offer assistance with planning tasks
- ☐ Y ☐ N Create a wedding-day emergency kit
- ☐ Y ☐ N Organize bridesmaids on wedding day

AT CEREMONY

- ☐ Y ☐ N Walk down the aisle directly before the bride (if no flower girl)
- ☐ Y ☐ N Adjust bride's train at altar
- ☐ Y ☐ N Hold bride's bouquet during the vows
- ☐ Y ☐ N Carry groom's wedding ring (if no ring bearer)
- ☐ Y ☐ N Walk in recessional with best man
- ☐ Y ☐ N Organize programs, toss petals, and so on
- ☐ Y ☐ N Sign marriage license as a witness

AT RECEPTION

- ☐ Y ☐ N Stand in receiving line
- ☐ Y ☐ N Help bride bustle her gown
- ☐ Y ☐ N Sit at head table next to groom
- ☐ Y ☐ N Make toast to the couple
- ☐ Y ☐ N Help "host" party (make introductions, get people dancing, and so on)
- ☐ Y ☐ N Dance with best man during first dance (if wedding party is involved)

best man

I want my best man to . . .

PREWEDDING

- ☐ Y ☐ N Help groom shop for formalwear
- ☐ Y ☐ N Coordinate formalwear fittings and payments
- ☐ Y ☐ N Plan the couple's shower and/or bachelor party
- ☐ Y ☐ N Spread word about couple's registry
- ☐ Y ☐ N Offer assistance with planning tasks
- ☐ Y ☐ N Arrange groomsmen's travel and lodging
- ☐ Y ☐ N Organize groomsmen on wedding day

AT CEREMONY

- ☐ Y ☐ N Stand at front with groom and other groomsmen as procession begins (or walk in, in a Jewish ceremony)
- ☐ Y ☐ N Carry bride's (or both) wedding ring(s)
- ☐ Y ☐ N Walk in recessional with bride's honor attendant
- ☐ Y ☐ N Sign marriage license as a witness
- ☐ Y ☐ N Give officiant his or her fee

AT RECEPTION

- ☐ Y ☐ N Stand in receiving line
- ☐ Y ☐ N Sit at head table next to bride
- ☐ Y ☐ N Serve as toastmaster, making first toast to couple
- ☐ Y ☐ N Dance with maid of honor during first dance (if wedding party is involved)
- ☐ Y ☐ N Help "host" party (make introductions, get people dancing, and so on)
- ☐ Y ☐ N Help direct vendors—caterer, photographer, band—as needed
- ☐ Y ☐ N Help groom give out final payments and tips to vendors
- ☐ Y ☐ N Collect gifts and gift checks brought to the reception

bridal party cheat sheet

bridesmaids

_____
_____
_____
_____
_____

I want my bridesmaids to . . .
PREWEDDING
- ☐ Y ☐ N Help bride shop for dress
- ☐ Y ☐ N Go on at least one bridesmaid-dress-shopping trip (except for out-of-town maids)
- ☐ Y ☐ N Go for fittings and alterations as needed
- ☐ Y ☐ N Help with wedding-planning errands
- ☐ Y ☐ N Help plan shower and/or bachelorette party

AT CEREMONY
- ☐ Y ☐ N Walk single file in the procession along with other bridesmaids
- ☐ Y ☐ N Stand in line in front of altar or stage, or sit in front pew with other bridesmaids
- ☐ Y ☐ N Walk in recessional paired with a groomsman

AT RECEPTION
- ☐ Y ☐ N Be announced at reception
- ☐ Y ☐ N Sit at head table

groomsmen

_____
_____
_____
_____
_____

I want my groomsmen to . . .
PREWEDDING
- ☐ Y ☐ N Help choose formalwear
- ☐ Y ☐ N Go for fittings and alterations as needed
- ☐ Y ☐ N Attend couple's shower
- ☐ Y ☐ N Help plan and attend bachelor party

AT CEREMONY
- ☐ Y ☐ N If also serving as an usher, stand at door ready to escort guests to their seats
- ☐ Y ☐ N Stand with groom, best man, and other groomsmen at the altar or stage as ceremony is about to begin
- ☐ Y ☐ N Stand in line or sit in front pew with other groomsmen during ceremony
- ☐ Y ☐ N Walk in recessional paired with a bridesmaid

AT RECEPTION
- ☐ Y ☐ N Be announced at reception
- ☐ Y ☐ N Sit at head table
- ☐ Y ☐ N Take part in first dance

flower girl

I want my flower girl to . . .
- ☐ Y ☐ N Attend shower with mother
- ☐ Y ☐ N Walk in processional

ring bearer

I want my ring bearer to . . .
- ☐ Y ☐ N Walk in processional with the wedding bands

parents cheat sheet: bride

mother of the bride

I want my mother to . . .

PREWEDDING

- ☐ Y ☐ N Host an engagement party (bride's family traditionally gets the first opportunity)
- ☐ Y ☐ N Help couple decide on sites and/or make other big planning decisions
- ☐ Y ☐ N Contribute to wedding budget
- ☐ Y ☐ N Help bride put together family's guest list
- ☐ Y ☐ N Offer suggestions for special family or ethnic ceremony traditions
- ☐ Y ☐ N Help bride shop for her wedding gown
- ☐ Y ☐ N Choose own wedding outfit (may consult with mother of the groom about formality)
- ☐ Y ☐ N Along with maid of honor and bridesmaids, plan and host a shower
- ☐ Y ☐ N On wedding day, help bride get ready
- ☐ Y ☐ N Travel to ceremony with her daughter and the father of the bride

AT CEREMONY

- ☐ Y ☐ N Be escorted by an usher (sometimes her son or husband) to her seat directly before the ceremony begins, if it's a Christian ceremony; in a Jewish ceremony, walk in procession with her husband and daughter and stand underneath huppah
- ☐ Y ☐ N Walk in recessional with her husband if it's a Jewish wedding; in a Christian wedding, be escorted out after wedding party

AT RECEPTION

- ☐ Y ☐ N Greet guests in receiving line
- ☐ Y ☐ N Be announced with her husband

father of the bride

I want my father to . . .

PREWEDDING

- ☐ Y ☐ N Along with his wife, host engagement party
- ☐ Y ☐ N Contribute to the wedding budget
- ☐ Y ☐ N Help couple decide on sites and/or make other big planning decisions
- ☐ Y ☐ N Help choose hotel for out-of-town guests and reserve a block of reduced-rate rooms, create maps to be included with invitations
- ☐ Y ☐ N Rent his own formalwear (ask couple if he's to coordinate with wedding party)
- ☐ Y ☐ N Help pick up out-of-town guests from the airport; may also arrange transportation to and from the wedding (vans, bus, and so on)
- ☐ Y ☐ N Travel to ceremony with his daughter

AT CEREMONY

- ☐ Y ☐ N Escort his wife to her seat directly before a Christian ceremony begins; walk his daughter down the aisle in a Christian ceremony; in a Jewish wedding, walk with his wife and daughter and stand under huppah
- ☐ Y ☐ N Walk in recessional with his wife in a Jewish wedding; in a Christian wedding, escort mother of the bride out after wedding party

AT RECEPTION

- ☐ Y ☐ N Greet guests in receiving line
- ☐ Y ☐ N Be announced with his wife
- ☐ Y ☐ N Make a welcoming speech

parents cheat sheet: groom

mother of the groom

I want my mother to . . .

PREWEDDING

☐ Y ☐ N Contact mother of the bride if the families are not acquainted

☐ Y ☐ N Attend (first) engagement party if the bride's family hosts one

☐ Y ☐ N Along with her husband, host an additional engagement party

☐ Y ☐ N Contribute to wedding budget

☐ Y ☐ N Help couple decide on sites and/or make other big planning decisions

☐ Y ☐ N Help groom put together guest list

☐ Y ☐ N Offer suggestions for special family or ethnic ceremony traditions

☐ Y ☐ N If close to the bride, help shop for her wedding gown

☐ Y ☐ N Choose own wedding outfit (may consult with mother of the bride about formality)

☐ Y ☐ N Along with her husband, plan and host the rehearsal dinner

AT CEREMONY

☐ Y ☐ N Be escorted by an usher (sometimes her son or husband) to her seat right before the mother of the bride is seated, if it's a Christian ceremony; in a Jewish ceremony, walk in procession with her son and husband and stand underneath huppah

☐ Y ☐ N Walk in the recessional with her husband, if it's a Jewish wedding; in a Christian wedding, be escorted out after bride's parents

AT RECEPTION

☐ Y ☐ N Greet guests in receiving line

☐ Y ☐ N Be announced with her husband

father of the groom

I want my father to . . .

PREWEDDING

☐ Y ☐ N Attend (first) engagement party if the bride's family hosts one

☐ Y ☐ N Along with his wife, host an additional engagement party for groom's side of the family

☐ Y ☐ N Along with his wife, contribute to wedding budget

☐ Y ☐ N Help couple decide on sites and/or make other big planning decisions

☐ Y ☐ N Rent his own formalwear (ask couple if he's to coordinate with the wedding party); attend fittings as needed

☐ Y ☐ N Along with his wife, plan rehearsal dinner

☐ Y ☐ N On wedding day, travel to ceremony with the groom and best man

AT CEREMONY

☐ Y ☐ N May escort his wife to her seat (right before the mother of the bride is seated) and before the Christian ceremony begins; if it's a Jewish wedding, walk down the aisle with his wife and son and stand under huppah

☐ Y ☐ N Walk in the recessional with his wife in a Jewish wedding; in a Christian wedding, escort his wife out after wedding party and bride's parents

AT RECEPTION

☐ Y ☐ N Greet guests in receiving line

☐ Y ☐ N Be announced with his wife

wedding party contact cheat sheet

maid/matron of honor _____   arrival ___ / ___ / _____

address/staying where _____   phone _____

_____   e-mail _____

bridesmaid _____   arrival ___ / ___ / _____

address/staying where _____   phone _____

_____   e-mail _____

bridesmaid _____   arrival ___ / ___ / _____

address/staying where _____   phone _____

_____   e-mail _____

bridesmaid _____   arrival ___ / ___ / _____

address/staying where _____   phone _____

_____   e-mail _____

bridesmaid _____   arrival ___ / ___ / _____

address/staying where _____   phone _____

_____   e-mail _____

bridesmaid _____   arrival ___ / ___ / _____

address/staying where _____   phone _____

_____   e-mail _____

best man _____

address/staying where _____

_____

arrival _____ / _____ / _____

phone _____

e-mail _____

groomsman _____

address/staying where _____

_____

arrival _____ / _____ / _____

phone _____

e-mail _____

groomsman _____

address/staying where _____

_____

arrival _____ / _____ / _____

phone _____

e-mail _____

groomsman _____

address/staying where _____

_____

arrival _____ / _____ / _____

phone _____

e-mail _____

groomsman _____

address/staying where _____

_____

arrival _____ / _____ / _____

phone _____

e-mail _____

groomsman _____

address/staying where _____

_____

arrival _____ / _____ / _____

phone _____

e-mail _____

family contact cheat sheet

bride's parents _____   arrival ____ / ____ / _____

address/staying where _____   phone _____

_____   e-mail _____

bride's parents (if there are divorced parents)   arrival ____ / ____ / _____

_____   phone _____

address/staying where _____   e-mail _____

_____

groom's parents _____   arrival ____ / ____ / _____

address/staying where _____   phone _____

_____   e-mail _____

groom's parents (if there are divorced parents)   arrival ____ / ____ / _____

_____   phone _____

address/staying where _____   e-mail _____

_____

bride's grandparents _____   arrival ____ / ____ / _____

address/staying where _____   phone _____

_____   e-mail _____

bride's grandparents _____   arrival ____ / ____ / _____

address/staying where _____   phone _____

_____   e-mail _____

groom's grandparents _____ arrival ___ / ___ / _____

address/staying where _____ phone _____

_____ e-mail _____

groom's grandparents _____ arrival ___ / ___ / _____

address/staying where _____ phone _____

_____ e-mail _____

other family vip _____ arrival ___ / ___ / _____

address/staying where _____ phone _____

_____ e-mail _____

other family vip _____ arrival ___ / ___ / _____

address/staying where _____ phone _____

_____ e-mail _____

other family vip _____ arrival ___ / ___ / _____

address/staying where _____ phone _____

_____ e-mail _____

guests' hotels contact cheat sheet

hotel _____

address _____

_____

contact _____

phone _____

fax _____

number of rooms in block reserved _____

reserved under name _____

group rate: $ ____ /night

guests _____

_____

_____

_____

_____

_____

_____

_____

_____

hotel _____

address _____

_____

contact _____

phone _____

fax _____

number of rooms in block reserved _____

reserved under name _____

group rate: $ ____ /night

guests _____

_____

_____

_____

_____

_____

_____

_____

_____

addresses or websites for local points of interest

_____

_____

_____

notes _____

_____

7

gift registry

Don't wait to register for gifts until the month before your wedding.
Friends and relatives will be looking to buy you gifts for events
like the engagement party and bridal shower, and many buy your
wedding gift the minute they get your save-the-date. You don't need
to complete your list right away, but at least have a selection for
guests to browse. Start with the traditional items like tableware and
linens (that's what Mom's friends will want to buy you), but feel free
to add camping gear and even parts of your honeymoon!

top registry tips

1 do it together

Hitting the stores together is essential. After all, the gifts are for both of you. First, to decide what you need, take inventory of the things you already have and see where the gaps are. Talk about the style of home you'd both like, and split up the final say (you could alternate items) to make it fair.

2 register for a range of gifts

China and flatware are just the beginning of the modern-day registry. Most stores have wedding registries now, so feel free to include whatever it is that will make your new house a home, be it electronics, appliances, or even camping equipment.

3 but think about how you live

Try to avoid filling your list with things you're never going to use. If you two aren't the formal-party types, then you probably won't need a crystal punch bowl. That said, just because you don't throw big sit-down dinners now doesn't mean you won't five to ten years from now. Also, be extra-sure before you register for anything that's monogrammed. You probably won't be able to return it.

4 check the store's return policies

Ask about a store's exchange/return policies. Many wedding registry retailers have amazing customer service.

5 make sure you hit all the price points

Register for items in a wide range of price points: under $50, under $75, under $100, etc.

6 spread the word

You won't get all those fabulous gifts if none of your guests know about your registry. Tell your attendants. Link from your website. Include it in your shower (but not wedding) invitation.

7 merge lists

Instead of having to access three different registry lists at three different stores, sign up for a universal online registry list. That way you can link and sync all of your registry items into one easy-to-access list.

8 update often

Update your registry with additional selections as products are purchased so that guests always have a variety of things to choose from. Aim to have at least twice as many items on your list as guests at your wedding.

9 think gift cards

Many stores allow you to register for them, and you can use them to buy the things you want and need later. If you're anxious for cash gifts, ask one or two close friends and immediate family members to politely spread the word.

10 say thanks

Open gifts as you receive them and record who gives you what. Thank-you notes for gifts received before the wedding should be sent within two weeks. Shoot for a month after the honeymoon for the others.

the knot TIP
Get the ultimate registry checklist at **TheKnot.com/registrychecklist.**

questions to ask
before you register

What's the return policy? Can you bring or send back duplicate gifts or anything you decide you don't want for a store credit or exchange? Is there a time limit after the wedding to return things?

_____

_____

_____

_____

Can gifts be shipped to an address you supply? (This is especially important if you're marrying in a town other than where you live.)

_____

_____

For smaller stores and boutiques: Is your registry accessible online? Can guests buy gifts online and have them shipped to your house?

_____

_____

How does the store keep track of what's purchased? How often is it updated? (It should be updated instantly to protect you against getting duplicate gifts.)

_____

_____

Will the person you're talking to be your store contact throughout the process? (Some places will assign you a registry consultant—someone who helps you make choices, keeps your list up-to-date, and so on.)

_____

_____

How long after your wedding is your registry list kept active? (It should be at least a year.)

_____

_____

Are there perks? Most stores will give you a discount on unbought items on your registry list (called a completion program). If that's the case, make sure you know how long after the wedding you can take advantage of it.

_____

_____

notes

_____

_____

_____

_____

_____

_____

guest list, invitations & wedding party

your wedding registries
contact cheat sheet

store name _____

website _____

consultant (if applicable) _____

e-mail _____

phone _____

store name _____

website _____

consultant (if applicable) _____

e-mail _____

phone _____

store name _____

website _____

consultant (if applicable) _____

e-mail _____

phone _____

notes _____

_____

_____

_____

_____

ASK CARLEY
gift etiquette

How do we let guests know we want cash instead of gifts?

Some guests will give you cash without your having to ask—it's traditional in many parts of the country and among many ethnic groups too (Chinese and Italian, to name but two). Otherwise, the best you can do is put your parents and wedding party on alert that if guests ask them what you'd most like for your wedding, they should say money. Then just cross your fingers! You should still register as a backup. Another strategy is to register for your honeymoon trip or for a down payment on a home. Use GR360.com and you can register for just about anything online. It's a gift registry that allows you to combine all of your registry items into one universal list. You can put anything on there—gift certificates, classes, artwork—so guests will still feel they're getting you something specific, and you get what you really need.

the other parties

You know you've got a wedding to plan, but you may not know that there are a slew of other celebrations that come into play as soon as you slip that engagement ring onto your finger. You certainly don't need to have each and every one of these parties, but you should be acquainted with the possibilities (and who's responsible for hosting).

party primer

engagement party

Who hosts: Tradition dictates that the bride's parents host the initial gathering, but couples stray from this all the time. The groom's parents can throw their own party, or both sets can come together to host one big fête. Your wedding party or close friends can even step in as hosts.

What: The purpose of the engagement party is pretty self-explanatory: It's to celebrate your engagement! This is also a great time to introduce your families if they haven't already met.

Where: Your parents' home, your favorite bar, a restaurant, on the beach . . .

When: A formal engagement party is usually scheduled two to four months after the big announcement. It shouldn't be any later than six months prior to the wedding date so that the two events aren't too close.

Guest list: There's just one rule: Everyone who is invited to the engagement party should ultimately be invited to the wedding.

bridesmaid luncheon

Who hosts: The bride.

What: A bridesmaid tea or luncheon to thank the gang for all the wedding prep they've helped with and also to get in some last-minute bonding. Usually on the mellow side, this girls-only get-together is an opportunity to swap stories and relax before the wedding day.

Where: Anyplace—at the hotel where you're staying, at a nearby restaurant, at a favorite café or tea salon.

When: The tea or luncheon is usually held a day or two before the wedding and sometimes on the big day. This timing works especially well if your bridesmaids are coming from all over and will be in town for only a few days.

Guest list: The maid of honor, bridesmaids, and flower girls. You might also include mothers, grandmothers, and other female family members.

rehearsal dinner

Who hosts: Traditionally, the groom's parents. But depending on who's paying for the wedding, the couple or the bride's family may decide to host.

What: As everyone is brimming with anticipation on the eve of the wedding, this celebratory dinner is filled with toasts and roasts.

Where: This can be casual or fancy. Many are held in hotel banquet rooms or at restaurants, with full-course dinners and desserts. Others are simply held at home.

When: It's held a day or two before the wedding—typically following the ceremony rehearsal.

Guest list: At the very least, it should include just the wedding party, very close family members, and the officiant. You might also invite out-of-towners.

welcome party

Who hosts: The couple or their parents.

What: This is more of a meet-and-greet event to get everyone familiar with one another before the wedding day.

Where: Many are held in the back room of a local restaurant, at the hotel where most guests are staying, or even in a close friend's or family's house.

When: It's usually held the day or evening before the wedding—when most guests have arrived.

Guest list: Usually everyone invited to the wedding is invited to the welcome party.

your wedding parties
cheat sheet

engagement party

date/time

host

guest list #

location

style notes

bridal shower

date/time

host

guest list #

location

style notes

bachelorette party

date/time

host

guest list #

location

style notes

bachelor party

date/time

host

guest list #

location

style notes

bridesmaid luncheon

date/time

host

guest list #

location

style notes

rehearsal dinner

date/time

host

guest list #

location

style notes

welcome party

date/time

host

guest list #

location

style notes

other

date/time

host

guest list #

location

style notes

party etiquette

What does a sample rehearsal dinner invitation look like, wording-wise?

It really depends on how formal you want to make it and how you plan to send out the invites (with the wedding invites or as a separate mailing?). Here's a general guide:

In anticipation of Susan & Joe's big day, please join us Friday, September 3, at 6 p.m. for great food, drinks, and celebration

BlackFinn Restaurant
19 E. 7th St., Cincinnati, Ohio

Please RSVP to Amanda at (513) 555-8106 or e-mail amanda@gmail.com

Can guests be invited to the engagement party but not the wedding?

You shouldn't expect someone to come to your shower or engagement party and give you a present if you're not planning to invite them to the wedding. It would seem like they were good enough to give you a gift but not good enough to celebrate with you on the big day. The engagement party is meant to be a party for the people closest to you, and they should all be invited to the wedding.

I'm having two wedding showers: a traditional bridal shower thrown by my aunts and a couple's wedding shower hosted by my future mother-in-law. One of my bridesmaids not-so-nicely implied that my fiancé and I were being greedy by having more than one bridal shower. But what can we do about it?

Your bridesmaid definitely wasn't being the best of friends when she made that comment. You and your fiancé should still certainly attend and enjoy both showers! However, if there is considerable overlap on the guest lists (or even if your attendants are planning on going to both events), it's probably a good move to send the message through the grapevine that you aren't expecting people who are attending both events to get you two major gifts. One of the main reasons people still feel uncomfortable about showers is because they're viewed as the to-be-weds fishing for gifts—you know you're not, obviously, because you've had these different family members offer to throw the parties. Even still, it can't hurt to make nice. You don't need to tell people formally—just let your wedding party or close relatives know that if they speak with anyone who will be attending both showers, they can hint that one gift is enough (of course, technically they don't have to get you anything, but rare is the shower attendee who is that bold!). That should be enough to assuage your guilty conscience.

9

your reception site

Try to book a year in advance—some places go a year and a half (or even two) ahead. Also make sure you have a good idea of the head count before you begin looking; a site for fifty is completely different from one for five hundred. If your caterer comes with your reception site, make sure to consult the checklists in chapter 10 before you make any final decisions.

reception site worksheet

Before you start reaching out to reception sites, check the box(es) under each heading that best describe(s) your image of your wedding location. It will give your search some focus.

style

☐ Big and grand

☐ Old-world, ornate

☐ Formal

☐ Modern, spare

☐ Intimate

☐ Fun, funky

☐ Rustic

☐ Casual

size

Must accommodate #_____ guests

location considerations

☐ Walking distance from ceremony

☐ Driving distance from ceremony site (within _____ minutes)

☐ Near public transit

☐ Close to guest hotels

features you want it to have

☐ Incredible interiors

☐ Breathtaking views

☐ Waterfront

☐ Surrounded by nature

☐ Rooftop

☐ Pool

services

☐ All-inclusive (site and food)

☐ Rentals (chairs, linens, cake table) included

☐ On-site coordinator included

☐ Kosher catering

outdoor space for any of the following

☐ Photos

☐ Ceremony

☐ Reception

☐ Cocktail hour

special requirements

☐ Disabled access

☐ Separate children's room

☐ Coat check

☐ Parking

☐ Tent space

☐ Do-it-yourself clean slate

☐ Ceremony space

☐ Dressing room

☐ Cocktail hour space

☐ On-site hotel rooms

☐ Other _____

venue budget $_____

finding your reception site

Research hotels, resorts, inns, country clubs, banquet halls, historic mansions, gardens, and more. Use **TheKnot.com/venuefinder** to start your search and narrow down options.

location _____

website _____

address _____

phone _____

manager _____

app't date ___ / ___ / ___ time _____

available dates ___ / ___ ___ / ___

rental fee $ _____

per-head costs $ _____ – $ _____

notes _____

_____

location _____

website _____

address _____

phone _____

manager _____

app't date ___ / ___ / ___ time _____

available dates ___ / ___ ___ / ___

rental fee $ _____

per-head costs $ _____ – $ _____

notes _____

_____

location _____

website _____

address _____

phone _____

manager _____

app't date ___ / ___ / ___ time _____

available dates ___ / ___ ___ / ___

rental fee $ _____

per-head costs $ _____ – $ _____

notes _____

_____

location _____

website _____

address _____

phone _____

manager _____

app't date ___ / ___ / ___ time _____

available dates ___ / ___ ___ / ___

rental fee $ _____

per-head costs $ _____ – $ _____

notes _____

_____

questions to ask reception site managers

Is the site available on your date (or a date acceptable to you)?

_____

_____

For how many hours will you have the site? Are there overtime fees?

_____

_____

How does the place charge—per head, by the hour, or a flat fee?

_____

_____

Can you bring in your own cake, florist, and so on, or must you use in-house staff? Is there a preferred vendor list? (See chapter 10 for more catering questions.)

_____

_____

Does the site have a liquor license? Can you bring in your own alcohol?

_____

_____

Can you see sample floor plans and/or visit when the room is set up for a wedding? Where does the band usually set up, the buffet usually go out, and so on?

_____

_____

What's the staff-to-guest ratio? (One or two waiters can't manage a party of two hundred.)

_____

_____

How many people will the space comfortably hold (not just official capacity, which may not include space for tables, and such)?

What will/can the facility provide?

☐ Cooking facilities

☐ Tables

☐ Chairs

☐ Dinnerware

☐ Linens

☐ Tent

☐ Additional lighting

☐ Dance floor

☐ Other _____

Does the room have adequate outlets (and power) for food-preparation equipment and lighting and audio needs?

_____

_____

Is there adequate lighting? How much customization is possible? Who will control the lighting during the reception?

_____

_____

Is there a dance floor, or must one be brought in? Can the site arrange it, or are you responsible for renting one? Is there an additional fee?

_____

_____

Are there any restrictions or rules about entertainment, decorations, and dress code?

_____

_____

How many bathrooms are there? Are there attendants? Do you need to tip them?

_____

_____

Is there ample parking? Are there attendants? Do you need to tip them?

_____

_____

If necessary, is there good security (and do you need to tip them)?

_____

_____

Will there be other weddings on the same day or at the same time?

_____

_____

Will the manager be present to oversee your reception to the end?

_____

_____

Can you get references of couples who had their weddings at the site?

_____

_____

Ask yourself: Is the manager flexible and willing to accommodate you?

_____

_____

Does the site have liability insurance?

_____

_____

ASK CARLEY
reception timeline

What does a typical reception timeline look like?
Draw up your own schedule based on this general timeline (times in brackets are one suggested example):
1. Cocktails are served. [6 p.m.]
2. Everyone is seated. [7 p.m.]
3. The DJ welcomes everyone. [7:15 p.m.]

4. The first dance may happen now. [7:20 p.m.]
5. First course is served. [7:30 p.m.]
6. Family/wedding party toasts happen. [8 p.m.]
7. The couple gives the thank-you toast. [8:30 p.m.]
8. Dancing begins. [9:30 p.m.]
9. Bouquet and garter tosses happen. [10 p.m.]
10. Last dance. [12:00 a.m.]

top reception tips

1 find the right color
If you're considering a certain theme and color palette for your party—say, a modern lounge-style cocktail party reception done in black and red—those gold-cord swag curtains are really going to wreck the effect. The site doesn't have to be done in the exact colors as your planned decorations, but the walls, carpets, chairs, and curtains shouldn't clash or conflict with your party's mood or theme.

2 know how to save
Marry in a less popular month (avoid June, September, and October). Consider a night besides Saturday—opt for a Thursday, Friday, or Sunday. Take advantage of your country-club membership or alumna status, or arrange for a city- or state-run site such as a public park or historic building.

3 the less conventional, the more complicated
If you choose a creative location such as a lighthouse or art gallery—or any location that doesn't do a lot of weddings—there will be more details to work out than if you choose a place that's known for wedding celebrations and has a planning brigade already in place.

4 gauge the privacy
If there will be other parties going on at your site at the same time as yours, you'll want to be sure it's not possible to hear music coming from other rooms and that there are enough bathrooms, coatrooms, and other facilities so things won't feel cramped. Ask if you can check things out at a time when several parties are taking place.

5 take care regarding cancellation
Your reception isn't likely to get canceled, but just in case, find out the exact date by which you'd have to cancel your reservation to get your money back. Also ask about what would happen in the event of extreme weather conditions.

6 weather the storm
If your site is outdoors, have an alternative location in mind in case of a blizzard, rain, or a heat wave.

7 do the hotel deal
If your reception is in a hotel where many guests will be booking rooms, the hotel banquet manager may have special rates or benefits since you're bringing in so much business. Don't be afraid to hint about perks, such as an upgrade to the honeymoon suite for you two.

8 beware the home wedding
It sounds like a great way to save, but renting everything that a banquet hall would supply can be costly in comparison. If you have your heart set on a tented wedding at home, consider essentials such as parking, restrooms, and a weather plan.

9 get a great view

Whether it's your city skyline or the rolling mountains out the window, locations with a view are a plus. If there's no view, look to the site's décor or architecture. Artwork, designer furniture, or an amazing chandelier that acts as the room's centerpiece will give your site that something extra.

10 take your time

It's critical that your other vendors have the information and access they need to get their jobs done. Make sure your site manager will let them view the space in advance, as well as give them access as early as they need it on your wedding day.

Elizabeth & Nathan

MODERN CLASSICS
APRIL 17
MILWAUKEE, WI

Elizabeth and Nathan's goal was to show off the best of their city to out-of-town guests. The Milwaukee Art Museum was the perfect modern backdrop. Cocktails were served in one of the galleries, followed by dinner in the main hall overlooking Lake Michigan. A preppy "Ralph Lauren" color palette—navy blue linens and centerpieces of bright-pink tulips (the iconic spring flower)—tied it all together.

booking the reception site

☐ Visit your favorite sites during an event to investigate acoustics, true capacity, and its decorated look (if at all possible).

Location

Date/time

Location

Date/time

☐ Ask your favorite sites to provide you with a list of two or three recent wedding-couple references.

☐ Call references and read reviews.

☐ Request the preferred vendor list.

☐ Finalize your decision and reserve the site. Make sure you have confirmation of your reservation in writing (e-mail or hard copy contract).

☐ Request a contract and review for critical points:

☐ Name and contact information for you and the vendor

☐ Date and time frame of your reception (the average dinner-and-dance reception is about four hours long, longer if it includes the ceremony)

☐ Exact names of specific room(s) to be used

☐ What time other vendors (florist, DJ, etc.) will be able to set up

☐ Approximate number of guests and number of tables to be set up (include a floor plan if possible)

☐ The name of the manager on duty during your reception

☐ An itemized list of what the site will provide (from waitstaff to linens, plus services such as coatroom and valet parking)

☐ Proof of insurance and liquor license

☐ Setup, cleanup, overtime, and any other fees

☐ Total cost (itemized)

☐ Deposit amount due

☐ Balance and date due

☐ Cancellation and refund policy

☐ Site manager's signature

☐ Sign the final contract.

☐ If your reception will be outdoors in a public place, file for a permit.

☐ Make a list of anything you'll need to rent (tent, tables, chairs, and so on) and look into rental companies; visit your site with your rental agent so she sees firsthand what you need (do all this about six to eight months before).

☐ Take pictures of the site to show to other wedding vendors.

☐ Ask for directions coming from various routes (you'll need this to include in invitations or to post on your wedding website). Drive them yourself.

☐ Meet with or call the site manager to discuss decorations and final menu decisions if you're working with in-house people, or to coordinate plans with outside caterers, florists, and other vendors (do this at least four months before).

reception contact
cheat sheet

reception site contact

name _____

address _____

_____

contact _____

phone _____

website _____

e-mail _____

room(s) and time reserved _____

_____

estimate $ _____

deposit $ _____

date paid ___ / ___ / ___

total cost $ _____

balance $ _____

date due ___ / ___ / ___

notes _____

_____

_____

reception site contact #2 (on-site
wedding coordinator, catering manager, chef)

name _____

phone _____

e-mail _____

reception site contact #3 (on-site
wedding coordinator, catering manager, chef)

name _____

phone _____

e-mail _____

wedding rentals contact

name _____

address _____

contact _____

phone _____

website _____

e-mail _____

lighting company contact

name _____

address _____

contact _____

phone _____

website _____

e-mail _____

your rental checklist

essentials

- ☐ Tent (square feet #_____)
- ☐ Dance floor
- ☐ Band stage
- ☐ Portable toilets #_____

tables

- ☐ Dining tables #_____ (to seat #_____ each)
  Square #_____
  Round #_____
  Long #_____
  Head tables #_____
- ☐ Chairs #_____
  Chair covers #_____
  Chair sashes #_____
- ☐ Bar/serving tables #_____
- ☐ Cake table

dinnerware

- ☐ Place settings #_____
- ☐ Hors d'oeuvre plates #_____
- ☐ Dessert plates #_____
- ☐ Serving pieces #_____
- ☐ Flatware sets #_____
- ☐ Extra forks, or other #_____

glassware

- ☐ Water glasses #_____
- ☐ White wine #_____
- ☐ Red wine #_____
- ☐ Bar glasses #_____
- ☐ Champagne flutes #_____

linens

- ☐ Reception table linens #_____
- ☐ Overlays #_____
- ☐ Cocktail table linens #_____
- ☐ Buffet table linens #_____
- ☐ Cake table linens #_____
- ☐ Other specialty linens #_____
- ☐ Napkins #_____

room décor

- ☐ Candelabras #_____
- ☐ Vases #_____
- ☐ Draping (your florist might also do this for you)
- ☐ Lighting (or you might go through a separate lighting company)
- ☐ Mirror (for behind the bar)
- ☐ Lounge furniture
  Couches #_____
  Chairs #_____
  Ottomans #_____
  Side tables #_____
  Coffee tables #_____
  High-top tables #_____
  Bar stools #_____

Estimate $_____

Deposit $_____

Date paid ____/____/____

Total cost $_____

Balance $_____

Date due ____/____/____

10

food & drink

Your wedding reception catering will probably be your largest wedding expense by far. It's also one of the things people will remember most about your event. Start making decisions in this arena early. Your caterer and reception site go hand in hand: If you're using an on-site caterer, carefully interview him before you book the reception site. If your caterer is independent, decide what to serve (brunch, lunch, heavy appetizers, dinner) soon so that you can determine the appropriate time to reserve the site.

your reception menu worksheet

Before you lock in a caterer, check the box(es) under each heading that best describe(s) your image of your wedding meal. If you have no idea, then leave it to discuss in your meetings with caterers.

meal

- ☐ Brunch
- ☐ Lunch
- ☐ Cocktail party
- ☐ Dinner
- ☐ Dessert only
- ☐ Late-night bites

cocktail-hour service

- ☐ Passed hors d'oeuvres
- ☐ Hors d'oeuvre tables
- ☐ Food stations (raw bar, sushi station, crepe table)

dinner service

- ☐ Family-style (passed around the table)
- ☐ Table service (waiter-served)
- ☐ Table service with white gloves (also called "Russian table service")
- ☐ French table service (plate prepared right next to the table)

flavor

- ☐ Continental (traditional)
- ☐ Ethnic _____
- ☐ Regional
- ☐ Thematic _____
- ☐ Seasonal
- ☐ Comfort foods

courses

- ☐ Starter
- ☐ Soup
- ☐ Dessert
- ☐ Amuse-bouche
- ☐ Appetizer
- ☐ Fruit and cheese
- ☐ Salad
- ☐ Pasta
- ☐ Palate cleanser
- ☐ Late-night snack

dietary restrictions

- ☐ Kosher % _____ or # _____ guests
- ☐ Vegetarian % _____ or # _____ guests
- ☐ Gluten-free % _____ or # _____ guests
- ☐ Dairy-free % _____ or # _____ guests
- ☐ Kid dinners % _____ or # _____ guests
- ☐ Other _____

catering budget

Total $ _____ divided by # of guests _____ = $ _____ per head

entrées

- ☐ Beef
- ☐ Pork
- ☐ Lamb
- ☐ Chicken
- ☐ Seafood
- ☐ Pasta
- ☐ Vegetarian
- ☐ Other food ideas

_____

dessert

- ☐ Cake only
- ☐ Plated desserts
- ☐ Dessert table

beverages

- ☐ Full bar
- ☐ Beer and wine only
- ☐ Specialty bar (vodka bar)
- ☐ Champagne toast
- ☐ Wine with dinner
- ☐ Wine pairings
- ☐ Signature cocktail
- ☐ Other (flights, tasting)

_____

top food & drink tips

1 ask for references

Don't choose your caterer based solely on your tasting. (It's easy to cook a good meal for two people. Checking references will let you know whether a caterer's skills extend to large groups.) Also, try at least two items for each course so you'll have an alternative.

2 find sneaky ways to save

Serve cocktails and appetizers instead of a full sit-down dinner. Cut down on dinner courses. Keep your menu simple. Avoid expensive ingredients (wild mushrooms, salmon steaks, and so on). Opt for pasta and chicken as entrées. Savor specialties of the season and region. Limit your bar.

3 try regional eats

Wedding food doesn't have to be boring. Find a caterer who serves (or is inspired by) festive cuisines such as Italian, Caribbean, Mexican, soul food, Cajun, or Greek. Just beware if there are picky eaters among your guests.

4 pass it around

Something in between a sit-down meal and a buffet, family-style offers a natural way to get tables of guests talking while creating a very festive and homey atmosphere. Each dish is delivered to the center of the table and guests pass them around the table.

5 be careful with restaurants

Serving a group of two hundred and preparing plates one by one are two different things. If you choose restaurant catering, make sure the place has wedding experience.

6 make a printed menu

If you're serving intriguing foods or using ingredients with special significance, explain them on a printed menu placed on each table. Make sure it matches your caterer's final list.

7 focus on service

Ask references whether the staff went the distance to ensure guests were served in an appropriately beautiful, friendly, fast, and attentive manner.

8 curb corkage fees

Purchase a set amount of liquor yourselves if you can; if bartenders simply open new bottles as needed, the cost per bottle opened (the corkage fee) can add up. Also, ask your bartender to watch over the bottle counting; it's easy to make a mistake.

9 rethink the beer and wine

People often limit drink options to beer and wine to help contain costs, but keep in mind that wine may well be pricier than hard alcohol—you'll get about five drinks out of a bottle of wine and twenty out of a bottle of alcohol.

10 serve a signature cocktail

A great way to add color and festive flair is to offer a special drink in addition to (or in lieu of) champagne. Consider something thematic: spiked eggnog or cider during winter; rum punch or piña coladas for island flavor; cosmopolitans or martinis for an urban, loungelike feel.

finding your caterer

Hotels, country clubs, and other large special-event facilities will likely have in-house caterers or preferred-caterer lists. Favorite restaurants may cater; be sure to browse all the caterers listed at **TheKnot.com/caterers** to research good ones in your area. Check ads in regional and/or national bridal or city magazines. You should also read reviews to find the highest-rated caterers in the area and make appointments with several caterers.

company _____

contact _____

website _____

phone _____

e-mail _____

address _____

price range $ _____

notes _____

_____

company _____

contact _____

website _____

phone _____

e-mail _____

address _____

price range $ _____

notes _____

_____

company _____

contact _____

website _____

phone _____

e-mail _____

address _____

price range $ _____

notes _____

_____

company _____

contact _____

website _____

phone _____

e-mail _____

address _____

price range $ _____

notes _____

_____

questions to ask caterers

Do they specialize in certain types of food? (Caterers should provide sample menus.)

_____

_____

Will they arrange for a tasting of the foods you might be interested in serving prior to your hiring them? (The answer should be yes.)

_____

_____

What is the average price range? Are costs itemized depending on the foods you choose, or is there an all-inclusive flat rate? Are there printed price sheets for food selections?

_____

_____

How involved are they in a typical reception—do they work like a wedding coordinator or banquet manager, cueing the band, telling the couple when to cut the cake, adjusting the schedule if guests aren't ready to sit down to dinner? (You'll need to find someone to fill this role—if not them, you'll need a coordinator.)

_____

_____

If your reception site can't, can they provide tables, chairs, linens, and dinnerware? (Ask to see linens, serving pieces, and the like to make sure they're acceptable to you.)

_____

_____

Do they set the tables and put out place cards and favors?

_____

_____

Will they provide waitstaff? How many would they recommend for the size of your wedding? What does the waitstaff wear? (Top caterers say they always use their own serving personnel, even if the site's staff is available.)

_____

_____

Where will food be prepared? Are there on-site facilities, or do the caterer and the site need to make additional arrangements? (If yes, is there an additional fee?)

_____

_____

Are they licensed by the state health department? (Very important!)

_____

Do they work with fresh food? Organic? Local?

_____

Do they provide alcohol, or is the bar the reception site's responsibility? (If you can provide it, is there a corkage fee? How and when do you get the alcohol to the caterer? If the caterer will provide it, do they have a wine list?)

_____

_____

building your own reception bar

These are averages. You know your crowd best, so buy accordingly
(so if your friends love to do tequila shots, one bottle won't be enough).

- ☐ Determine how much of each type of alcohol you need (following estimates are open-bar amounts for 100 people):
  - ☐ White wine (18 bottles)
    Total _____
  - ☐ Red wine (10 bottles)
    Total _____
  - ☐ Beer (2–3 cases)
    Total _____
  - ☐ Whiskey (1–2 liters)
    Total _____
  - ☐ Bourbon (1–2 liters)
    Total _____
  - ☐ Gin (2 liters)
    Total _____
  - ☐ Scotch (3 liters)
    Total _____
  - ☐ Rum (2 liters)
    Total _____
  - ☐ Vodka (6 liters)
    Total _____
  - ☐ Tequila (1 liter)
    Total _____
  - ☐ Dry and sweet vermouth (2 bottles each)
    Total _____
  - ☐ Tonic and club soda (1 case each)
    Total _____

- ☐ Cranberry juice (2 gallons)
  Total _____
- ☐ Orange and grapefuit juice (1 gallon each)
  Total _____
- ☐ Other (for specialty cocktail)
  Total _____
- ☐ Champagne toast: 18 bottles (assumes 6 glasses per bottle, 1 glass per person)
  Total _____
- ☐ Wine for dinner: 50 bottles (assumes 4–6 glasses per bottle, 2 glasses per person)
  White wine total _____
  Red wine total _____

- ☐ Find a liquor discounter or wholesaler. (If your caterer doesn't have a referral, search online.)
- ☐ Send a list of needs to two liquor suppliers and ask for a detailed price quote (including tax and delivery charges, if any).
- ☐ Find out when you need to deliver liquor to the caterer.

- ☐ Order and pay with a credit card.
- ☐ Make sure you get an invoice that includes:
  - ☐ A list of all items and amounts ordered
  - ☐ What items (if any) will arrive chilled
  - ☐ The delivery date and time
  - ☐ The exact delivery address
- ☐ Confirm that the caterer or bartender is supplying tools (shakers, ice tongs).
- ☐ Confirm that the caterer or bartender will do all prep work (for example, cutting limes).
- ☐ Confirm that the caterer is renting enough glasses for the drinking you have envisioned (for example, if you're having a champagne toast, you will need a flute for each guest).
- ☐ When the alcohol is delivered, expect to tip $10 to the delivery person.

TO-DO CHECKLIST
hiring your caterer

- ☐ Arrange for tastings (if you didn't have one on your first visit).

  Caterer _____

  Date ___ / ___ / ___ Time _____

  Caterer _____

  Date ___ / ___ / ___ Time _____

  Caterer _____

  Date ___ / ___ / ___ Time _____

- ☐ Ask each caterer to draw up a proposal, including
  - ☐ Cost per person
  - ☐ Options for hors d'oeuvres, appetizers, entrées, and accompaniments
  - ☐ Exactly what the price includes: alcohol, rentals, gratuities
  - ☐ Service and presentation style (how the food will be laid out)
  - ☐ Less expensive alternatives, if this is something you've discussed

- ☐ Call references and ask the following questions:
  - ☐ Ask for some background: how many guests, the venue, the menu
  - ☐ Was the meal good, hot, and well-presented?
  - ☐ Were guests served and tables cleared efficiently?
  - ☐ Any surprises on the final menu or final bill?

- ☐ Reserve your favorite caterer. E-mail them to confirm your wedding date (and create a paper trail).

- ☐ Finalize menu decisions:
  - ☐ Hors d'oeuvres _____
  - ☐ Appetizers _____
  - ☐ Salad or soup course _____
  - ☐ Entrée(s) _____
  - ☐ Side dishes _____
  - ☐ Cheese course _____
  - ☐ Drinks _____
  - ☐ Dessert _____
  - ☐ Cake _____
  - ☐ Other _____

- ☐ Finalize per-person price $ _____

- ☐ Request a contract.

- ☐ Review for critical points and revise as needed:
  - ☐ Name and contact information for you and the vendor
  - ☐ Date, starting time, and length of your reception
  - ☐ Location of reception, including the exact name of the room
  - ☐ Date the caterer needs a final head count
  - ☐ Staff: waiter-to-guest ratio, number of bartenders
  - ☐ Type of service (cocktails, buffet, tea, dessert, seated meal)
  - ☐ If buffet, how you'll be charged (by number of guests or by plate count)
  - ☐ A specific menu (you may make alterations to this menu later)
  - ☐ Acceptable food substitutions (in case of unavailability on wedding day)

(CONTINUES)

- ☐ Liquor: what kinds, how much
- ☐ Cake: layers, flavor, ornamentation
- ☐ Rentals: what's included (tablecloths, napkins, dishes, tables, and so on)
- ☐ Your point person
- ☐ Proof of license and liability insurance
- ☐ The approximate number of guests
- ☐ Costs per person (three levels: adult, child, vendor)
- ☐ Detailed accounting of extra fees:
  - ☐ Sales tax
  - ☐ Rentals
  - ☐ Fees for extra waiters
  - ☐ Gratuities
  - ☐ Delivery

- ☐ Kitchen fee
- ☐ Bar or corkage fee
- ☐ Cake-cutting fee
- ☐ Overtime rates
- ☐ Total estimated cost of the service
- ☐ Deposit amount due
- ☐ Balance and date due
- ☐ Cancellation and refund policy
- ☐ Caterer's signature
- ☐ Sign the final contract.
- ☐ If any special facilities or equipment is needed at the reception site, schedule a meeting with the caterer and site manager to discuss and make arrangements.

caterer contact cheat sheet

caterer _____

contact/point person _____

website _____

phone _____

e-mail _____

address _____

phone _____

order _____

delivery information _____

_____

estimate $ _____

deposit $ _____   date paid _____

total cost $ _____

balance $ _____   date due _____

notes _____

_____

_____

_____

_____

11

your wedding cake

Your wedding cake should certainly taste great, but it should also turn heads as the centerpiece of the reception. Have it designed to match your wedding style, echoing your colors, flowers, or theme. You can even have it created to match your dress, with similar detailing or motifs. Try to book your cake baker six to eight months before the wedding. Just keep in mind that noted designers—the kind featured in national or big-city magazines—may be booked far in advance.

wedding cake worksheet

style

☐ Traditional ☐ Classic white ☐ Simple ☐ Quirky
☐ Ornate ☐ Round ☐ Modern ☐ Colorful
☐ Tall and grand ☐ Petite and understated ☐ Square ☐ Cupcakes

# of tiers _____

cake should be

☐ A major reception focal point ☐ The primary dessert ☐ A photo opportunity

ornamentation options

☐ Fresh flowers ☐ Patterned ☐ Coordinated to the dress ☐ In keeping with
☐ Sugar flowers ☐ Textured ☐ Coordinated to the theme or culture
☐ Simple bands ☐ Smooth and simple invitations ☐ Seasonal

on top

☐ Monogram ☐ Flowers ☐ Unique piece (a small ☐ Thematic piece
☐ Couple topper ☐ Family cake topper (your vintage vase, piece of (butterflies, bicycles)
  grandparents', parents') jewelry) ☐ Nothing

cake flavors _____

icing

☐ Fondant ☐ Buttercream

cake fillings _____

_____

color and theme ideas _____

_____

of slices _____ (will likely equal
of guests)

cake budget $ _____

---

ordering a groom's cake?
☐ Yes ☐ No

Groom's cake flavor ideas _____
_____
_____

Groom's cake theme ideas _____
_____
_____

of slices _____
(often smaller; allot for half the # of guests)

groom's cake budget $ _____

top wedding cake tips

1 size it up

Three standard tiers will probably serve a hundred guests; you'll likely need five layers for two hundred guests or more (these are guidelines; ask your cake designer for exact numbers). If you'll have a dessert table or other sweets in addition to cake, consider a cake sized for half your number of guests (the servings will be a little smaller).

2 get flavor pricing

Unless you simply can't decide, don't order different flavors by layer. Variety could cost you— and guests don't generally get to choose anyway!

3 find ways to save

Order a smaller cake that's exactly what you want and several sheet cakes of the same flavor to be cut in the kitchen. Stay away from complex tiers, handmade sugar flowers, and custom cakes involving special molded shapes.

4 get creative with your topper

Riff on your wedding theme, consider your hobbies, include pictures, or make it yourself. Make sure that all decorative elements that are not edible are removed before serving.

5 mind your flowers

If you use fresh flowers, make sure they are sturdy and can withstand an evening under the lights without wilting. Your florist will know the best options and may even add stem reinforcements to keep flowers from looking droopy. Also, triple-check with your florist that the flowers have not been sprayed with pesticides.

6 know your frosting

If you're getting married outdoors in a hot climate, stay away from whipped cream, meringue, and buttercream icing, which melt!

7 skip the diy route

It's a nice personal touch to have your grandmother or mom bake your cake, but this works better for the other, smaller events (like the rehearsal dinner). Baking for a hundred or more is a feat of engineering best left to the professionals.

8 delivery details

Cake delivery will take a little coordination. Complex cakes may not necessarily be delivered ready to go. Make sure there's time and space for assembly to take place. Refrigeration may also be required.

9 mind your cake table

A round table is perfect for round cakes, but a square design may look better displayed on a rectangular table. Next, pick out linens that will highlight the color of the cake. Finally, don't hide your wedding cake in the corner. Have it set on risers or near the entrance of your reception.

10 freezer burn

Eating the top tier of your cake on your first anniversary sounds far better than it tastes— believe us. Instead, indulge on your two-week anniversary—and treat yourself to a fresh cake in the same flavor after you've survived the first year.

finding your cake baker

To find cake designers and bakeries, ask newlywed friends or your caterer, florist, or photographer; use a favorite bakery; or work with the in-house designer at your reception site. Research cake looks you like (try magazines, cake articles online, and wedding-cake books). Copy, rip out, or print out pictures to bring with you and browse hundreds of cake photos at **TheKnot.com/bakers,** and make appointments with several cake designers/bakeries.

cake bakery/designer name

_____

website _____

phone _____

e-mail _____

address _____

referred by _____

app't date ___ /___ /___ time _____

price estimate $ _____

notes _____

_____

cake bakery/designer name

_____

website _____

phone _____

e-mail _____

address _____

referred by _____

app't date ___ /___ /___ time _____

price estimate $ _____

notes _____

_____

ASK CARLEY
wedding cake

What is a "cake-cutting fee"?

If you use a cake designer who is not affiliated with your reception site and/or caterer, the establishment may charge this additional fee of $1.50 or more per person to cut and serve the cake. It's an incentive for you to use their in-house baker (and not be charged an extra fee).

What's a groom's cake?

Groom's cakes are a Southern tradition. Traditionally, they were rich chocolate cakes. These days, both cakes can be whatever flavor you'd like. Go theme-crazy with the groom's, having it made in the shape of a football, a checkerboard, or anything else.

questions to ask
cake bakers

Will he or she create a custom cake, or are there specific styles to choose from? Look at photos and actual cakes, if possible. (Bring pictures if you have a custom cake style in mind.)

_____

_____

What ingredients are used—fresh fruits or purees, Italian buttercream, farm-fresh butter, kosher? (This may or may not be crucial to you, but the better the ingredients, the better a cake will taste! It could also cost more.)

_____

_____

What are the options for cake flavors and fillings? Do they work in fondant or buttercream?

_____

_____

Is there a baker and a designer, or does one person do the entire cake, from batter to sugar flowers? How many people work with the designer? (You'll get an idea of the time it takes the shop to put out a cake. Whether it's a single person or a team of people, however, should have no bearing on quality.)

_____

_____

Does he or she do sugar flowers? Can he or she do custom motifs or sculptures from sugar?

_____

_____

If you want to garnish your cake with fresh flowers, will he or she work with your florist?

_____

Are cakes priced by the slice or by the cake? Are different flavors or fillings different prices? Will there be extra labor costs if the cake is one-of-a-kind or complex? (Ask for a price list.)

_____

_____

Does he or she provide cake stands? Or can the cake be presented on what it is delivered on? (Ask to see a picture.)

_____

_____

Does the price include the top cake tier, or is it extra? (Our favorite bakers include the top tier—the one many couples save for their first anniversary—for free.)

_____

_____

Is he or she licensed by the state health department? (Very important!)

_____

How does delivery work? How much does it cost? (Unless you're having a very small cake, you will want the baker to deliver. He or she has trained delivery staff and refrigerated trucks.)

_____

_____

cake baker contact cheat sheet

cake designer/baker _____

cake baker name _____

website _____

phone _____

e-mail _____

address _____

description of cake _____

_____

number of people to feed # _____

estimate $ _____

deposit $ _____ date paid _____

total cost $ _____

balance $ _____ date due _____

ordering your cake

☐ If possible, try it out. Attend tastings or ask for sample slices.

☐ Book your favorite cake designer and e-mail to confirm; include your wedding date.

☐ Finalize decisions as to

   ☐ Cake flavor _____

   ☐ Fillings _____

   ☐ Icing _____

   ☐ Decorations _____

   ☐ Number of tiers _____

   ☐ Cake topper _____

   ☐ Number of guests to feed _____

☐ Request a contract or an invoice and review for the following critical points:

   ☐ Name and contact information for you and the vendor

☐ Wedding date, time, and location

☐ When, how, where (complete address of site), and by whom the cake will be delivered

☐ A detailed description of the cake ordered (including all items listed above)

☐ A list of anything you're renting (plastic cake tiers, cake stand, and so on)

☐ Delivery and setup fees

☐ Total price

☐ Deposit amount due

☐ Balance and date due

☐ Cancellation and refund policy

☐ Cake designer's signature

☐ Sign the final contract or invoice.

the dress

Your dress is the wedding's true centerpiece. Remember these three things: (1) Start shopping as soon as possible, as in nine to eleven months (or more) before the wedding—it'll take the pressure off the process. Place your order according to the time suggested by the manufacturer. (2) You'll have found it when you look in the mirror and feel absolutely fabulous. (3) Consider your accessories carefully—they need to complement your overall look.

your wedding dress worksheet

Before you get lost in all of your dress options, try to get an idea of what you imagine yourself wearing. As you begin to look around (the ten-thousand-plus-image wedding gown guide on **TheKnot.com/gowns** is the best place to begin), try to identify the features you like most.

style (check all that apply)

☐ Formal
☐ Informal
☐ Classic
☐ Traditional
☐ Ornate

☐ Spare and simple
☐ Unusual
☐ Nonwhite (blush, lavender, yellow)

☐ Modern
☐ Glam/red carpet
☐ Sexy
☐ Flowy

☐ Fairy-tale-esque
☐ Romantic
☐ Tailored
☐ Lots of coverage

shape

☐ Ball gown
☐ Sheath
☐ A-line
☐ Mermaid/trumpet

neckline

☐ Strapless
☐ Jewel neck

☐ Sweetheart
☐ Sabrina (bateau)

☐ Off-the-shoulder
☐ Scoop neck

☐ Halter

length

☐ Floor-length
☐ Knee-length
☐ Chapel-length
☐ Cathedral-length

sleeves

☐ Short or cap sleeves
☐ Long sleeves
☐ No sleeves

fabric elements

☐ Lace
☐ Beading

☐ Ruffles
☐ Floral appliqués

☐ Pickups (bustled fabric throughout the skirt)

---

the knot TIP
Need gown inspiration? See thousands of dresses by style, designer, and price at **TheKnot.com/dressfinder.**

color

- ☐ White
- ☐ Ivory
- ☐ Champagne
- ☐ Cream, candlelight
- ☐ Other _____

accessories

- ☐ Long veil
- ☐ Minimal veil
- ☐ Tiara
- ☐ Hairpins
- ☐ Pumps
- ☐ Sling-backs
- ☐ Strappy sandals
- ☐ Purse/clutch
- ☐ Long gloves
- ☐ Short gloves
- ☐ Wrap or shawl
- ☐ Bolero
- ☐ Fur stole
- ☐ Cape or coat

jewelry

- ☐ Necklace
- ☐ Bracelet
- ☐ Earrings
- ☐ Other _____

wedding dress and accessories budget $ _____

Asha & Bryson
BALLROOM ROMANCE
APRIL 17
ATLANTA, GA

Asha never would've considered the dress she ended up buying if her best friend hadn't suggested it. But the minute she tried it on (at a Lazaro trunk show), she knew it was perfect. The dress—covered in airy, shredded organza petals with a pearl ribbon belt and a chapel-length train—fit Asha and Bryson's downtown Atlanta ballroom setting.

dress & accessories

top wedding dress tips

1 match your location

Tie your look to your wedding location. If you're having a traditional ceremony with a formal reception, opt for a classic, timeless gown style (like an A-line or a ball gown with a square neckline). If you're marrying in the sand, a flirty tea-length gown is the ultimate nontraditional wedding attire.

2 size it up

Forget about your regular dress size. Bridal sizes run small, and each wedding dress manufacturer actually has its own sizing chart. A knowledgeable bridal salon consultant will know how designers' dresses are supposed to fit. Know, too, that every dress needs alterations. When it's altered correctly, you should be able to move comfortably and the dress should stay in place.

3 research your religion

Many churches and synagogues consider bare shoulders disrespectful. Ask your officiant, and get yourself a wrap or a bolero jacket if you simply must have a strapless gown.

4 shop around

Don't buy the first dress you try on, even if you love it. Give yourself options and the time to think. Because gowns are custom-made, once you've ordered, there's no turning back. Expect strict cancellation and refund policies.

5 shop at an authorized store

If you buy a gown from a shop not authorized to sell that designer's line, there's no guarantee that your dress is going to arrive on time, if at all.

If you're unsure whether a shop is authorized, call the manufacturer. (Find wedding dress designer contact info at TheKnot.com/gowns.)

6 keep an open mind

The most elegant gowns often have the least presence or appeal on the hanger. Try various silhouettes; you never know what's going to flatter you. Experienced bridal salon consultants can literally size you up the minute you walk in the door and know what dresses will show off your assets.

7 shop during off hours

Take time off during the week, day or evening, to shop—you'll get more of the salespeople's time and attention.

8 don't travel with an entourage

One to three fellow shoppers is sufficient. Too many opinions will just overwhelm you.

9 size matters

If you are a voluptuous bride, find a salon that carries samples in a size to suit you (many do these days). There are also designers who specialize in styles for larger sizes.

10 try a trunk show

If you find a designer you like, visit during these in-store events featuring a specific designer (or a representative of a manufacturer) and his or her entire line. You'll get an opportunity to see and/or purchase every dress in the line, not just the styles that the store chose to sell that season.

finding your bridal salon

Research all the stores in your area. Ask girlfriends where they shopped for their dresses and browse the ads in wedding magazines to see which stores in your area sell dresses you like. Nearly every salon nationwide also has a list. Go to **TheKnot.com/bridalsalons,** where you can also see photos of the designer lines they carry, and make appointments at several bridal salons.

store name _____

consultant _____

website _____

phone _____

referred by _____

app't date ___ / ___ / ___ time _____

address _____

designers they carry _____

_____

_____

_____

_____

_____

price range $ _____

store name _____

consultant _____

website _____

phone _____

referred by _____

app't date ___ / ___ / ___ time _____

address _____

designers they carry _____

_____

_____

_____

_____

_____

price range $ _____

favorite designers and styles _____

_____

_____

_____

dress & accessories

questions to ask
bridal salons

What size sample dresses are available to try on? (Most stores only have samples in a size 8 or 10.)

_____

_____

Can you look through the dresses yourself, or does the salesperson bring them out? (Many stores will let you look through samples to get an idea of what you like; then the salesperson brings you gowns to try on based on your preferences.)

_____

_____

Which silhouette do they recommend for your figure? Which neckline?

_____

_____

Does the store carry the designers you're interested in?

_____

Does the store carry dresses in your price range?

_____

Does the store have shoes and bustiers to try on with gowns, or must you bring your own? (Find out when you call to make your appointment.)

_____

_____

If you like a dress that the store doesn't carry, will they order a sample for you to try on? (Just keep in mind that you may then be obligated

to buy the dress. Find out if the store is able to borrow a sample from the manufacturer.)

_____

_____

How long does it generally take for a dress to come in after it's been ordered? (It usually takes three to four months.)

_____

_____

Can the order be rushed, if necessary?

_____

Does the store carry headpieces and other accessories (purses, gloves, shoes)? If not, can they suggest other places to shop?

_____

_____

Can you get a written alteration estimate when you order your dress? (It's difficult to tell exactly what will need to be altered until the dress comes in, but ask for a basic price list. Alterations should be a flat fee, or even included.)

_____

_____

Does the store carry bridesmaid dresses as well? What about flower girl dresses? If your bridesmaids order their dresses through this store, do you receive a discount?

_____

_____

bridal salon
contact cheat sheet

wedding dress & accessories

store _____

contact _____

address _____

phone _____

website _____

store hours _____

dress designer _____

style number _____

price $ _____

consultant _____

alteration estimate $ _____

accessories (with prices) _____

total cost $ _____

deposit $ _____   date paid _____

balance $ _____   date due _____

date when the dress will be in _____

dates of fittings

    first ____ / ____ / ____   second ____ / ____ / ____   third ____ / ____ / ____

notes _____

_____

_____

your wedding dress, fittings & accessories

your dress

- ☐ Choose your gown. If possible, also select your headpiece now.

- ☐ Get measured (bust, waist, and hips—and possibly shoulders, based on the dress style).

- ☐ Decide what size to order. Ask to see the manufacturer's sizing chart yourself; choose the size that fits your largest measurement.

- ☐ Request a letter of agreement or review your invoice for the following critical points:
  - ☐ Contact info for you and the salon
  - ☐ Your wedding date
  - ☐ A detailed description of your dress, including
    - ☐ Designer or manufacturer name
    - ☐ Style number
    - ☐ Size ordered
    - ☐ Color
    - ☐ Fabric
    - ☐ Any special requests (extra length, etc.)
  - ☐ Date the dress will be delivered to the store
  - ☐ Descriptions of any accessories you order
  - ☐ Total price, itemized for the dress, headpiece, alteration estimate, and any other accessories or services (such as steaming)
  - ☐ Deposit amount due
  - ☐ Balance and date due
  - ☐ Cancellation and refund policy
  - ☐ Salesperson's/owner's signature
- ☐ Keep a copy of the invoice.

your fittings & accessories

- ☐ Schedule a first fitting (probably within three to six months).

  Date _____ / _____ / _____ Time _____

- ☐ About a month after you order, call the shop to confirm your delivery date.

- ☐ Make a list of all the accessories you'll need, and start to purchase them (you'll want lingerie and shoes in time for your first fitting):
  - ☐ Bustier/bra
  - ☐ Garter
  - ☐ Slip
  - ☐ Stockings
  - ☐ Petticoat
  - ☐ Crinoline
  - ☐ Pumps
  - ☐ Sandals
  - ☐ Wrap
  - ☐ Purse
  - ☐ Gloves
  - ☐ Jewelry

- ☐ When the dress comes in, try it on and check it over carefully. Make sure it's the style you ordered and that nothing is damaged.

- ☐ Have your first fitting. (The salesperson or seamstress will pin the dress in places where you need it taken in.)

- ☐ Schedule a second fitting (when you'll try on the altered dress to make sure it fits).

  Date _____ / _____ / _____ Time _____

- ☐ If you haven't yet, decide on a hairstyle.

- ☐ At your second fitting, determine whether your dress fits you properly. (If it does, the store will press it for you and you can take it home.)

- ☐ If more alterations are necessary, schedule a third fitting.

  Date _____ / _____ / _____ Time _____

wedding dresses

Which dress silhouettes flatter which figures?

You should definitely try on several different silhouettes to find the one that looks best on you, but here are some general guidelines:

Petite: Consider a columnlike sheath or a high-waisted dress to add length. Look for something simple with detail around the shoulders to bring the focus up to your face. An open neck is also flattering to a petite woman. Avoid a wide border around the skirt hem.

Full-figured and curvy: Try dresses with a basque waist—a natural waist with a V front and full skirt, which has a slimming effect on the waist and hips. A high-waisted dress with a low neckline also flatters curves.

Thick/undefined waist: Try on an Empire-waist dress—a small bodice with a slender skirt that falls in a slight A-line from right below the bustline. That said, if you have a large chest or hips, you probably want to stay away from Empire-waist dresses.

Short-waisted (or any shape): Try princess, or A-line, dresses, with seams running from the shoulders to the hem but with no seams on the waist, for a long, slim look. This style works on just about every figure.

Boyish figure: A traditional ball gown may be for you, fitted through the bodice to the waist with a full skirt. It's a very feminine shape that adds curves.

This is my second wedding. Can I wear white?

Yes, of course! White simply represents joy and celebration and is just as much your terrain as it is a first-time bride's. If you don't feel comfortable in an elaborate ball gown, go for a simpler dress with a modest headpiece. Whether to wear a veil is up to you.

I'm trying to lose a lot of weight in time for my wedding. I don't want to have to buy a size that fits me now or get a style that would flatter my current shape. Do I wait until I lose the weight to shop for my dress?

You could wait until a month before the wedding and buy a gown off the rack at a discount store or at a department store, but then you risk not finding the wedding gown you really want.

To address a larger concern, though, making your wedding date the deadline to lose a certain number of pounds may not be the best idea. That just puts extra pressure on you during the already stressful planning period. You shouldn't stop eating healthy foods and exercising. But keep in mind that you're marrying the man you love, and he loves you for *you*—not for your weight!

dress & accessories

your hair & makeup worksheet

First, you'll need to answer a question: Will you go to the professional,
or will the professional come to you?

hairstyle (check all that apply)

☐ Updo   ☐ Chignon

☐ Down and natural   ☐ Half pulled back

☐ Curls   ☐ Short and styled

accessories (check all that apply)

☐ Hairpins   ☐ Tiara

☐ Veil

☐ Other _____

makeup style (check all that apply)

☐ Natural   ☐ Bold lips

☐ Glamorous   ☐ Glowing

☐ Bold eyes

☐ Other _____

who will get hair done
(check all that apply)

☐ You

☐ Your bridesmaids

☐ Moms

☐ Grandmothers

☐ Others _____

who will get makeup done
(check all that apply)

☐ You

☐ Your bridesmaids

☐ Moms

☐ Grandmothers

☐ Others _____

ASK CARLEY
accessories

What's the etiquette for veils?

How much veil to wear for your ceremony is up to you—some brides opt for a clip, headband, or fresh flowers instead; others go for yards of fabric and a "blusher" veil to go over their face. Many brides choose to wear their veil during the reception (minus the blusher, of course), but others find it unwieldy. You might want to consider a veil attached to the headpiece with a clip, which can be easily removed without disturbing your hairstyle for the party.

questions to ask
hair & makeup artists

Does she have a portfolio of her work you can examine?

_____

_____

Does he have a list of references you can call?

_____

_____

How does he charge—by the hour? By the person?

_____

_____

How many weddings does she do in one day? (Will yours be the only one, or will she be rushed to get to another wedding?)

_____

_____

hair & makeup contact
cheat sheet

hairstylist _____

phone _____

e-mail _____

website _____

address _____

_____

hours _____

date of appointment(s) ____ /____ /____

time _____

total cost (plus tip) $ _____

makeup artist _____

phone _____

e-mail _____

website _____

address _____

_____

hours _____

date of appointment(s) ____ /____ /____

time _____

total cost (plus tip) $ _____

6-month wedding beauty countdown

This step-by-step beauty schedule will have you looking fabulous come wedding day.

6 months before

☐ Want to grow your hair out or try a new color or cut? Experiment now.

☐ Get serious about your skin care. Start a good cleansing, nutrition, and stress-relief regimen.

☐ If you don't already, start exercising! A few sessions with a trainer may help jump-start your routine.

☐ Find and meet with a makeup artist for a trial run, or get a makeover at a department store counter and purchase any products you need now (so you have time to practice).

1–2 months before

☐ Take your veil to your hairstylist to try out wedding day dos.

☐ Have your eyebrows professionally shaped. Why not? It's your wedding!

☐ Test out at-home masks or a salon facial. (Don't risk an allergic reaction on your wedding day.)

☐ Moisturize! Soft and silky elbows, hands, and feet are a marriage must.

☐ Want a sparkling smile? Cut down on tea and coffee, and try a whitening toothpaste or look into professional whitening.

2 weeks before

☐ Eat right. Load up on fruits and veggies; nix the salt and fat.

☐ Drink lots of water and exercise, exercise, exercise.

☐ Get your final haircut or trim.

☐ Touch up your hair color.

☐ Do a full hair trial before your final dress fitting. (If you're not happy, now's the time to speak up!)

1 week before

☐ Avoid overindulging in salty snacks and alcohol at those fab prewedding parties.

☐ Have a bikini wax and a final eyebrow shaping.

☐ Remind your man to get his final trim.

☐ Get a massage (if you can afford it; if not, ask him to do the deed—and give him one too).

☐ Get a final facial. (Do not wait until the day before to do this!)

1 day and counting

☐ Drink lots of water! (Have we made ourselves perfectly clear?)

☐ Deep-condition your hair.

☐ Get a professional manicure and pedicure.

☐ Shave and exfoliate, particularly if you're going bare-legged.

☐ Take a long, relaxing bath and moisturize after.

the bridesmaid dresses

You can shop for your bridesmaids' gowns as soon as you've decided on your dress. The options are almost limitless when it comes to picking a bridesmaid dress: You can go for matching designer dresses, buy them off-the-rack, or mix and match. Take at least one attendant with you when you shop—you'll need her as an advocate for everyone else. It will take a few months to coordinate sizes, for the dresses to come in, and for alterations to be done. Start as soon after the seven-month mark as you can.

bridesmaid dress shopping worksheet

style (check all that apply)

☐ Formal

☐ Informal

☐ Traditional

☐ Trendy

☐ Short sleeves

☐ Sleeveless

☐ Floor-length

☐ Tea-length or shorter

☐ Mix-and-match pieces (varying necklines, styles)

☐ Ornate, beaded

☐ Simple, unadorned

how much do you want them to match?

☐ Identical styles

☐ Same color and fabric, different styles (necklines, hemlines)

☐ Same color family but different styles and fabrics

☐ Other _____

accessories (which do you want them to have?)

☐ Wraps/sweaters/coats

☐ Shoes (matching or just coordinated)

☐ Purses

☐ Jewelry

colors

_____

_____

budget per dress (consult bridesmaids) $ _____

notes

_____

_____

_____

_____

_____

_____

_____

top bridesmaid dress tips

1 comfort is key

Even if you fall in love with the perfect pair of fuchsia four-inch stilettos to match the ribbon trim on the dress, don't subject your girls to that torture. If you're choosing the shoes for them, comfort should be the top priority.

2 be open to variety

Your bridesmaids don't have to look like clones. Consider choosing a designer and color and letting them each make their own choice from the line.

3 color-coordinate

If you're dead set on matching maids, it's a good idea to order all the dresses at the same store so they'll be created from the same batch of fabric. (Same goes for shoes.)

4 choose wearable colors

A wedding party in, say, black is your best (and, frankly, easiest) option for an evening affair. Nobody can complain about the color—and who can't use another black dress? All-white (or ivory) bridal parties are also all the rage.

questions to ask while shopping for bridesmaid dresses

What size sample dresses are available to try on?

_____

_____

Are there color-swatch charts, so you can see what colors different styles are available in?

_____

_____

Can you and your bridesmaids look through the dresses yourselves, or are they shown by a salesperson?

_____

_____

How long does it generally take for the dresses to come in after they've been ordered? (The average is one to two months.)

_____

_____

Can the order be rushed, if necessary?

_____

_____

If you ordered your wedding dress through the same store, will your bridesmaids (or you) be offered a discount or free alterations?

_____

_____

finding your
bridesmaid dress store

Research stores (the salon where you bought or shopped for your wedding gown, a wedding warehouse or outlet-type store, the dress section of your favorite department store) and ask bridesmaids for any off-limits styles or colors. Remember, you want them to coordinate, but you also want them to feel comfortable! The best way to get a sense of all the styles out there is to browse the thousands of bridesmaid dress styles at **TheKnot.com/bridesmaiddresses.**

make appointments at several salons
(preferably including the one you're already working with)

store name/designer

contact person

website

phone

address

referred by

app't date ____ /____ /____ time _____

notes

favorite designers and styles

store name/designer

contact person

website

phone

address

referred by

app't date ____ /____ /____ time _____

notes

favorite designers and styles

bridesmaid dress contact cheat sheet

You may want to give each bridesmaid her own copy of this sheet.

name _____

contact _____

address _____

_____

phone _____

website _____

store hours _____

dress description(s) and style number(s) _____

_____

date dresses will be in _____

deposit $ _____ date paid _____

total cost $ _____

balance $ _____ date due _____

Annamarie & Ryan

AFTERNOON ELEGANCE
JUNE 18
RICHMOND, VA

"I loved my bridesmaids' look!" Annamarie says. "I was so jealous I didn't get to wear their dress, too!" To capture their little white chapel relaxed afternoon wedding vibe, she chose knee-length coral dresses and strappy gold heels for her seven bridesmaids. The guys looked the part in brown suits and champagne ties.

bridesmaid dresses, alterations & accessories

bridesmaid dresses

☐ Along with your maids, decide on a dress (or several styles).

☐ Get measurements—bust, waist, and hips—from all bridesmaids (have out-of-towners send you theirs).

☐ If you're ordering them for everyone, figure out what sizes to order. Ask to see the manufacturer's sizing chart yourself, and have your bridesmaids choose the size that fits their largest measurement (they can always be altered down).

☐ Before you pay, review your invoice for the following critical points (bridesmaids may each do this separately; you may supervise orders for out-of-towners):

  ☐ Name and contact information for you (or the bridesmaid) and the vendor

  ☐ Your wedding date

  ☐ A detailed description of the dress or dresses, including

    ☐ Designer or manufacturer name(s)

    ☐ Style number(s)

    ☐ Size(s)

    ☐ Color(s)

    ☐ Fabric(s)

    ☐ Number of dresses ordered

    ☐ Any special requests (different sleeves and so on)

    ☐ Date the dresses will be delivered to the store

  ☐ Descriptions of any accessories you order (for example, shoes to match)

  ☐ Total price

  ☐ Deposit amount due

  ☐ Balance and date due

  ☐ Cancellation and refund policy

  ☐ Salesperson's/owner's signature

☐ Sign and keep the invoice.

alterations & accessories

☐ Based on when the dresses are expected to come in, have all local bridesmaids schedule a fitting.

☐ About a month after ordering, call the shop to reconfirm the delivery date (or check on your order online).

☐ When the dresses arrive, you or the maid of honor should go see them to make sure they're the style(s) you ordered and that nothing is damaged.

☐ Have your maid of honor pick up any out-of-towners' gowns (she'll likely have to pay the balance; ask the other attendants to reimburse her, or you) and ship them to each maid. They should have fittings done at a tailor or dress shop near them.

☐ Shop for and choose a shoe style. Let your bridesmaids know where to get the shoes, or purchase them yourself and send them out. (Or just give them guidelines and let them choose their own shoes.)

☐ Touch base with all maids to be sure they pick up their fitted gowns and pay the balance.

bridesmaid dress worksheet

Once you've found the perfect bridesmaid dresses, it's time to accessorize your ladies. Use this worksheet to figure out who's wearing what. Hint: If you're requiring them to wear matching pieces, it's a good idea to give them as a gift.

maid/matron of honor

name

☐ ordered dress   /   /

☐ alterations app't   /   /

☐ dress received   /   /

shoes

jewelry

notes

bridesmaid

name

☐ ordered dress   /   /

☐ alterations app't   /   /

☐ dress received   /   /

shoes

jewelry

notes

bridesmaid

name

☐ ordered dress   /   /

☐ alterations app't   /   /

☐ dress received   /   /

shoes

jewelry

notes

bridesmaid

name

☐ ordered dress   /   /

☐ alterations app't   /   /

☐ dress received   /   /

shoes

jewelry

notes

bridesmaid dress etiquette

How do I tell my bridesmaids that they have to pay for their own dresses? Two of them have never been in a wedding before.

The fact that they haven't been in a wedding before should actually make it easy—they don't know any different, right? Just explain that when someone stands up in a wedding, they're responsible for paying for what they'll wear. If you think cost is going to be an issue, do all you can to choose a dress that's reasonably priced—or consider letting the attendants choose their own dresses, so they'll get to decide how much to spend.

Do the bridesmaid dresses need to coordinate with what the groomsmen wear?

Your wedding party's outfits should have the same level of formality—for example, if your maids are wearing casual summer sundresses, the guys can't be in tuxes. Beyond that, if the guys will wear cummerbunds or vests, you'll probably want to choose a color that complements the bridesmaid dresses. Often the men's only color is in their boutonnieres—and since those flowers will likely complement the bride's bouquet (and, by association, the bridesmaids' flowers), everyone should match.

How closely do the bridesmaid dresses have to match the bride's gown?

Generally, the attendants should wear dresses that match the formality of the bride's dress. You wouldn't want to put the maids in sundresses when the bride's in a formal gown, but as far as the actual style of the dress and the details (neckline, sleeves, and other elements), they do not have to match exactly, if at all.

A few of my attendants are cranky because they don't like the dress I've chosen for them. Shouldn't they just wear what I want them to?

You stress about how you look in a dress, right? Why should your friends be any different? While it's almost impossible to make everyone 100 percent happy, you should still shoot for that. Be honest. Is your heart set on a sleek sheath dress you saw on a skinny model in a magazine, but your attendants are mostly curvy and not that tall? Did you choose sea foam simply because you want it to be your wedding color, without any regard for the fact that it makes most women feel uncomfortable? Be sensitive to your attendants' varying body shapes and coloring. Ask their opinions, and be flexible.

My matron of honor is pregnant, but it's really expensive to make alterations to the bridesmaid dress we picked out. Is it okay for her to wear a different style?

Not only is it okay, it's the best way to go. To accommodate her growing baby bump, choose an Empire-waist dress, with a high waistline (right under the bust) and an A-line skirt that doesn't constrict her hips, waist, or stomach.

the formalwear

If you're going the traditional route, your formalwear decisions will be dictated by the time and formality of the affair. If you're renting, don't wait until the last minute. Reserve all formalwear around the four- or five-month mark, and pick it up a few days before the wedding. Hint: That's a great best man job.

formalwear worksheet

the groom

☐ Tuxedo   ☐ Suit   ☐ Military   ☐ Other _____

☐ Single-breasted   ☐ Double-breasted

☐ Tie, pattern/color _____   ☐ Vest, pattern/color _____

☐ Bow tie, pattern/color _____   ☐ Shirt, pattern/color _____

☐ Cummerbund, pattern/color _____   ☐ Suspenders, color _____

☐ Shoes, style/color _____   ☐ Socks, style/color _____

☐ Cuff links

Color

☐ Black   ☐ Gray/charcoal   ☐ Brown   ☐ White/cream (linen)

☐ Navy   ☐ Other _____

groom's formalwear budget $ _____

groomsmen

☐ Tuxedo   ☐ Suit   ☐ Military   ☐ Other _____

☐ Single-breasted   ☐ Double-breasted

☐ Tie, pattern/color _____   ☐ Vest, pattern/color _____

☐ Bow tie, pattern/color _____   ☐ Shirt, pattern/color _____

☐ Cummerbund, pattern/color _____   ☐ Suspenders, color _____

☐ Shoes, style/color _____   ☐ Socks, style/color _____

☐ Cuff links

Color

☐ Black   ☐ Gray/charcoal   ☐ Brown   ☐ White/cream (linen)

☐ Navy   ☐ Other _____

Formalwear source

☐ Rental   ☐ Closet   ☐ Purchase

groomsmen's formalwear budget (each) $ _____

top formalwear tips

1 know what it costs
The average tuxedo rental is $150, depending on the style and where you rent from. Rental generally includes a jacket, trousers, a shirt, a vest or cummerbund, studs, cuff links, and a tie. If you have reason to wear a tuxedo at least two or three times a year, it might pay for you to buy one for your wedding—a nice one will run $500 to $1,500 and up.

2 know how to save
Wear a basic black, nondesigner tux. A formal tailcoat or daytime cutaway coat will cost more. If your wedding is semiformal, the groom and groomsmen can wear nice suits they already own. If you're all renting from the same place, you should get a discount, or the groom's rental may be free.

3 stand out in style
The groom should have a slightly different look than the groomsmen. Consider a different color of vest or cummerbund, a different tie or shirt style or color, or a slightly different jacket style (or a white dinner jacket for the groom with the groomsmen in black).

4 get comfortable
To make sure your formalwear fits correctly, check the following: (1) With your arms at your sides, the jacket hem is not longer than the tips of your fingers; (2) your shirt just peeks out from the jacket sleeves; (3) the jacket sleeves hit the tops of your hands; (4) your pants touch the heels of your shoes and have a small fold in front over the shoes; (5) you can squat without splitting seams; and (6) you can comfortably lift your arms to just below shoulder height.

5 match it
If you and your bride are determined to match the men's accessories (vests, ties) to the bridesmaid dresses, bring a fabric swatch when you go to the formalwear store or tie shopping.

6 wear the right white
If the bride is wearing a pure-white dress, the guys should not wear ivory, and vice versa. It'll be noticeably different.

7 order all at once
Rent all the groomsmen's suits from the same store. Ask the shop for measurement cards to send to out-of-towners. Make sure they have time to visit the formalwear store a day or so before the wedding for a final fitting.

8 pay their way
Groomsmen pay for their own rentals, but it's a good idea to place one big order and get paid back. Don't rely on everyone to make their own arrangements—it may not happen.

9 avoid tux shortages
If your wedding is around the holidays or during the high seasons for weddings or proms, visit the formalwear store six months in advance.

10 return rules
Arrange for someone to return all the formalwear to the shop after the wedding—the best man is a good candidate.

finding a formalwear shop

For formalwear rentals, check out chain or independent tuxedo stores or department stores and check out **TheKnot.com/formalwear.** Some bridal salons also rent formalwear.

make appointments at several stores

salon name _____

contact person/consultant _____

website _____

phone _____

address _____

referred by _____

app't date ___ / ___ / ___ time _____

$ _____ rating: ☆ ☆ ☆ ☆ ☆

notes _____

_____

_____

_____

_____

_____

_____

_____

salon name _____

contact person/consultant _____

website _____

phone _____

address _____

referred by _____

app't date ___ / ___ / ___ time _____

$ _____ rating: ☆ ☆ ☆ ☆ ☆

notes _____

_____

_____

_____

_____

_____

_____

_____

questions to ask formalwear stores

Does the store have formalwear in stock for you to try on, or can you only look at styles on mannequins?

_____

_____

What's the starting price? Are there package deals if you rent a certain number of tuxedos?

_____

_____

What's included in a full rental (accessories, pressing, other services)?

_____

_____

Can you buy a tuxedo? What's the starting price?

_____

_____

Are there on-site and/or same-day alterations?

_____

_____

formalwear store contact cheat sheet

name
_____

contact
_____

website
_____

address
_____

_____

phone
_____

store hours
_____

type and amount of formalwear ordered

_____

_____

pickup date _____ / _____ / _____

return date _____ / _____ / _____

total cost $ _____

deposit $ _____   date paid _____

balance $ _____   date due _____

renting the formalwear

☐ Along with the best man, try on styles you like and decide whether the groom's outfit will be slightly different from the rest of the men's.

☐ Make final decision(s) on your formalwear.

☐ Get measured, and have the best man and other groomsmen come in to do the same; have out-of-town groomsmen send in their measurements.

☐ Decide what size(s) to order. Ask to see the manufacturer's sizing chart yourself. Choose the size that fits each groomsman's largest measurement.

☐ Review your invoice for the following critical points:

    ☐ Name and contact information for you and the store

    ☐ Your wedding date

    ☐ Complete description of what you're renting _____

    ☐ Designer or manufacturer name(s) _____

    ☐ Groom _____

       Size _____

    ☐ Groomsman _____

       Size _____

    ☐ Groomsman _____

       Size _____

    ☐ Groomsman _____

       Size _____

☐ Groomsman _____

   Size _____

☐ Style numbers _____

_____

☐ Colors _____

_____

☐ Fabrics _____

_____

☐ Accessories (vests, cuff links, shoes) ____

_____

_____

_____

☐ Number of tuxes ordered _____

☐ Pickup date _____ / ___ / _____ Time _____

☐ Pickup date _____ / ___ / _____ Time _____

☐ Total price $ _____

☐ Late-return fee $ _____

☐ Deposit amount due $ _____

☐ Balance $ _____

☐ Due date _____ / ___ / _____

☐ Cancellation and refund policy_____

_____

_____

☐ Salesperson's signature

☐ Sign the invoice.

☐ If you'll wear any accessories (tie, cuff links) that don't come with your rental, purchase them.

formalwear

Should the groom wear a tux at our daytime wedding?

Ultimately, he can wear whatever you want, but bear these guidelines in mind:

Daytime: If your entire wedding will happen when the sun is up, tuxes are out. For an ultraformal affair, men traditionally sport a morning suit. If the event is formal but not over-the-top, focus on gray stroller coats or formal suits in shades to suit the season. If it's semiformal, men can simply wear nice suits, and in warm weather, if the setup is casual, they can even wear sports jackets and trousers.

Evening: If your reception will begin after six p.m. (five thirty is fine, too—and in winter you can stretch it even earlier), you can officially don eveningwear. If this is a super-formal occasion, get ready for white tie, complete with black tailcoats (the top hats and canes can stay in the closet). A formal evening wedding calls for black tie—that means tuxedos or James Bond–style white dinner jackets. If it's a semiformal affair, tuxedos are appropriate, or the guys can just wear nice dark suits.

Is it okay for the groom to take his jacket off at the reception?

Keep it on during cocktails so everyone can see how handsome he looks! It's fine to remove the jacket for the dance floor later (after the first dance). If he wears a vest, consider a style with a back instead of one with an adjustable waist and open back—he'll still look put-together without his jacket.

Tuxes seem so boring. Are there any ways to dress one up and make it unique?

Vests and patterned ties make a standard tux special. Formal suits (in brown or gray) can also be a nice alternative to the standard tux, depending on how formal (or not) you want to go. Or keep it classic on the cover and go crazy with fun socks, cool boxers, and novelty cuff links (all make great groomsmen gifts).

I want the guys to wear tuxes, but I don't want my guests to have to go out and rent them. How do I let them know they don't have to?

Include the phrase "black tie invited" or "black tie optional" on your invitations. This tells male guests that the men in the wedding party are going to be decked out in tuxes and that they're invited to wear them as well, but that dark suits are just as appropriate. It also clues women in to the fact that they should wear evening gowns or cocktail dresses.

notes

your ceremony

The ceremony is the wedding. For some, a favorite family officiant or house of worship drives the ceremony. For others, it's built around a beloved location. Be aware in advance that if you want a religious service, there are rules involved—not just about where the ceremony takes place and how it's structured, but also about the words, music, people, and rituals involved. Make sure to okay everything with your priest, minister, or rabbi. If you'll have a civil (secular) ceremony, feel free to be as creative as you'd like.

ceremony style worksheet

ceremony

☐ Religious

☐ Civil (secular)

☐ Long and symbolic (for example, full Mass)

☐ Short and sweet (just vows)

religion(s)

_____

_____

location

☐ House of worship ☐ Unique indoor venue

☐ Reception venue ☐ Outdoors

guests in attendance

☐ Just the couple and family

☐ All reception guests

☐ Reception guests and congregation

attendants

for bride _____

for groom _____

other VIPs _____

rituals (check all that apply, and add those from your own religion)

☐ Vow exchange (traditional or original vows?)

☐ Ring exchange

☐ Moment of silence

☐ Readings

☐ Offering to ancestors

☐ Unity ritual (candle)

☐ Performance

☐ Marriage contract

☐ Wine-sharing ritual

☐ Special song

jewish rituals

☐ _Ketubah_ (marriage contract)

☐ _Huppah_ (wedding canopy)

☐ _B'deken_ (veiling of the bride)

☐ _Sheva brachot_ (seven blessings)

☐ Breaking the glass

☐ _Yichud_ (a moment alone after the ceremony)

☐ _Tish_ (speeches)

remarriage (with children) rituals

☐ Family vow exchange

☐ Exchange of rings

☐ Family unity ritual between new parent and children

other rituals or requirements of your culture or religion _____

_____

vow or reading ideas (separate from rituals)_____

_____

ceremony budget $ _____

top ceremony tips

1 keep vows simple

If you write your own vows, keep them relatively short and personal (but not too personal), and decide ahead of time if you'll memorize them or carry a written version down the aisle. You don't want to forget your lines!

2 make a program

Ceremony programs aren't required, but they're a great place to list and thank your wedding party and close family. If you're including special religious or ethnic traditions, a program is a perfect way to explain them.

3 schedule a rehearsal

Don't worry too much about processional and recessional order; your officiant will make sure everyone knows where to stand, when to walk, and when to sit.

4 invite your officiant

Send your officiant and her spouse an invitation to your reception; plan to seat them with your parents or at another family table. Especially if your officiant has known your family for a long time, you'll definitely want her there. Many officiants decline, but they'll appreciate the gesture.

5 include both families (and faiths)

Early in the process, listen to both families' views and expectations for your wedding day. You and your sweetie should then decide how to proceed—and discuss your choices with your families. Be honest with everyone from the start so they know what you're planning and why.

ASK CARLEY
ceremony

Do we have to do a receiving line?

No, but there are certainly a number of benefits to having a receiving line because it ensures that you'll spend one-on-one time with each and every guest on your wedding day. It's customary to have one if you've invited fifty guests or more, but if you're having a hundred and fifty or more, consider it a must. The line can form casually at the ceremony site after the wedding (as people are leaving), or at the cocktail hour or reception as guests are arriving. Pick a spot (ahead of time) where there's room for people to form a line while they wait. Many couples include their parents—the bride's parents are first, then the bride and groom, then the groom's parents—or it can be just the two of you.

ceremony

finding your ceremony site & officiant

First you need to find a ceremony site. Religious options include notable local churches, your current church or temple, your parents' church or synagogue, a house of worship you're interested in joining as a married couple, a military chapel (if one or both of you is in the service), and a college chapel (at your alma mater). For civil sites, the sky's the limit.

If you have no connection to a specific church but want an officiant of a certain denomination to perform your ceremony, ask a friend (anyone can get ordained online through organizations like the Universal Life Church) and search listings at **TheKnot.com/officiants.** Try nondenominational or interfaith officiants. Make appointments with several sites and/or officiants (unless you're marrying in your own house of worship and the decision is a given).

ceremony site _____

officiant _____

address _____

website _____

phone _____

fee $ _____

app't date   /   /   time _____

available dates   /   /   /   /

notes _____

_____

ceremony site _____

officiant _____

address _____

website _____

phone _____

fee $ _____

app't date   /   /   time _____

available dates   /   /   /   /

notes _____

_____

ceremony site _____

officiant _____

address _____

website _____

phone _____

fee $ _____

app't date   /   /   time _____

available dates   /   /   /   /

notes _____

_____

ceremony site _____

officiant _____

address _____

website _____

phone _____

fee $ _____

app't date   /   /   time _____

available dates   /   /   /   /

notes _____

_____

questions to ask ceremony site managers & officiants

Is the site/officiant available on your date?

_____

_____

Does the site/officiant charge a standard fee?
Is it a donation to the house of worship, or a
specific amount paid to the officiant?

_____

_____

If you want to marry at a nonreligious site, is a
religious officiant willing to marry you there?

_____

_____

Is the sanctuary or other ceremony space large
enough for the approximate number of guests
you're planning to invite?

_____

_____

What will the site supply (prayer books, aisle
runner, huppah, candelabra)?

_____

_____

What are the restrictions on music?

_____

_____

Must you use the site's in-house musicians?

_____

_____

If your ceremony will be outdoors in a public
place, do you need a permit?

_____

_____

Can you write original vows?

_____

_____

Do you choose the readings?

_____

_____

Is prewedding counseling required?

_____

_____

Will the officiant conduct a gay wedding?

_____

_____

Will the officiant be your primary contact?

_____

_____

ceremony

officiant & site contact sheet

officiant _____

website _____

phone _____

fee $ _____

time _____

available dates   /   /   /   /

ceremony site _____

website _____

phone _____

fee $ _____

time _____

available dates   /   /   /   /

christian processional lineup

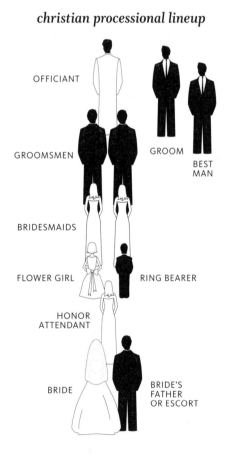

OFFICIANT

GROOMSMEN

GROOM

BEST MAN

BRIDESMAIDS

FLOWER GIRL

RING BEARER

HONOR ATTENDANT

BRIDE

BRIDE'S FATHER OR ESCORT

jewish processional lineup

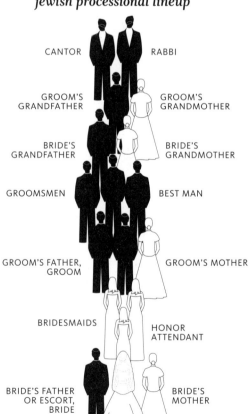

CANTOR

RABBI

GROOM'S GRANDFATHER

GROOM'S GRANDMOTHER

BRIDE'S GRANDFATHER

BRIDE'S GRANDMOTHER

GROOMSMEN

BEST MAN

GROOM'S FATHER, GROOM

GROOM'S MOTHER

BRIDESMAIDS

HONOR ATTENDANT

BRIDE'S FATHER OR ESCORT, BRIDE

BRIDE'S MOTHER

booking your ceremony site

- ☐ Choose your site and officiant and confirm in writing; include your wedding date and time.

- ☐ If you'll need to rent anything, contact a rental company (or ask your florist):
  - ☐ Ceremony chairs # _____
  - ☐ Huppah
  - ☐ Columns or arch
  - ☐ Candelabra
  - ☐ Wire stands for flowers

- ☐ Research ceremony readings and religious or ethnic ceremony customs and traditions; set up a meeting to discuss with your officiant.

- ☐ Ask your officiant for a copy of his standard ceremony so that you can make changes to suit you (if allowed).

- ☐ Schedule prewedding counseling (if required) Date(s) and time(s) to meet with officiant

  _____

  Date(s) and other pertinent info about group meetings and/or weekends away

  _____

- ☐ Finalize the overall structure and elements of the ceremony (readings, lighting candles).

- ☐ Determine which of the following ceremony items you will need; start shopping or make arrangements to have them made:
  - ☐ *Ketubah* or other marriage contract (for example, Quaker)
  - ☐ Yarmulkes
  - ☐ Unity candle (or sand for a sand ceremony)
  - ☐ Aisle runner
  - ☐ Ring pillow
  - ☐ Programs
  - ☐ Parasols
  - ☐ Something to toss
  - ☐ Flower girl basket
  - ☐ Other elements (such as a broom for the jumping of the broom or crowns for a Greek Orthodox ceremony)

  _____

- ☐ If you'll write your own vows, start working on them at least two months before; consult your officiant if you need help.

ceremony

your ceremony music worksheet

What do you want your ceremony music to sound like? Decide on a style
and then put together your budget below.

type (check all that apply)

☐ Recorded music (DJ)

☐ Pianist/organist

☐ Classical guitarist

☐ String quartet

☐ Harpist

☐ Vocalist

☐ Other music groups

specific songs you may want to consider/include

_____

_____

_____

hours of music needed _____

ceremony music budget $ _____

Courtney & Ethan
FORMAL ROMANTIC
FEBRUARY 19
SAN FRANCISCO, CA

Armed with style buzzwords
like *black-tie* and *modern*,
Courtney and Ethan picked
city hall, an iconic San
Francisco spot, as their
venue. They decked it out
in a color combo of black
graphite and deep, reddish
persimmon, and included
a few Art Deco details to
convey a timeless vibe. As
another nod to the city,
a print of the Bay Bridge
appeared on many of the
day's paper elements.

finding your
ceremony musicians

Get names and browse options at **TheKnot.com/musicians**,
then make appointments with several musicians, vocalists, or groups.

musician name(s)/company
_____

website
_____

e-mail
_____

phone
_____

referred by
_____

app't date   /   /   time
_____

type of music
_____

price estimate $ / hr
_____

notes
_____
_____
_____

musician name(s)/company
_____

website
_____

e-mail
_____

phone
_____

referred by
_____

app't date   /   /   time
_____

type of music
_____

price estimate $ / hr
_____

notes
_____
_____
_____

musician name(s)/company
_____

website
_____

e-mail
_____

phone
_____

referred by
_____

app't date   /   /   time
_____

type of music
_____

price estimate $ / hr
_____

notes
_____
_____
_____

musician name(s)/company
_____

website
_____

e-mail
_____

phone
_____

referred by
_____

app't date   /   /   time
_____

type of music
_____

price estimate $ / hr
_____

notes
_____

the knot TIP
Need ceremony song ideas? Find
hundreds by genre at
TheKnot.com/ceremonysongs.

questions to ask
ceremony musicians

Have the musicians played many weddings?

_____

Can you hear the musicians play or sing? Request a sample.

_____

_____

Are the musicians familiar with the music you want? Must you supply sheet music?

_____

_____

What equipment is required (music stands, microphones, speakers, and so on)?

_____

_____

How much room will the musicians need?

_____

If you're hiring a vocalist or additional musicians to be accompanied by the church organist or other in-house musicians, will everyone be available to rehearse?

_____

_____

What will the musicians wear?

_____

_____

How much setup time is needed?

_____

What is the musicians' fee for a wedding? Must you pay travel expenses as well?

_____

_____

ceremony musicians contact
cheat sheet

musician name(s)/company _____

website _____

phone _____

e-mail _____

address _____

estimate $ _____

deposit $ _____ date paid _____

total cost $ _____

balance $ _____ date due _____

hiring your
ceremony musicians

☐ Book your musicians. E-mail or get a written contract to confirm your reservation; be sure to include your wedding date and time.

☐ Finalize decisions as to:

   ☐ Instrument(s) to be played

   _____

   ☐ Music to be sung or played

    Prelude

    _____

    _____

    Processional

    _____

    _____

    During ceremony

    _____

    _____

    Recessional

    _____

    _____

    Postlude

    _____

    _____

☐ Request a contract or letter of agreement and review for the following critical points:

   ☐ Name and contact information for you and the vendor

   ☐ Your wedding date, address of location, and exact arrival time

   ☐ The name(s) of, and the instrument(s) played by, the musician(s)

   ☐ Any equipment you or the site will supply

   ☐ The names of the selections to be played

   ☐ Any agreements for you to supply sheet music

   ☐ What the musician(s) will wear

   ☐ The number of hours the musician(s) will play

   ☐ Total cost

   ☐ Deposit amount due

   ☐ Balance and date due

   ☐ Cancellation and refund policy

   ☐ Musician's signature

☐ Sign the final contract.

your wedding rings

Devise a plan for your wedding rings. They don't have to match perfectly, but it's a good idea to order them sooner rather than later so that you can be sure you get what you want in time for the ceremony. Research reputable jewelers at **TheKnot.com/jewelers.**

☐ Choose material
- ☐ White gold
- ☐ Platinum
- ☐ Yellow gold
- ☐ Rose gold
- ☐ Silver
- ☐ Graphite
- ☐ Titanium
- ☐ Other _____

☐ Choose style
- ☐ Embedded gems
- ☐ Plain band
- ☐ Ornate
- ☐ Custom-designed
- ☐ Fitted to engagement ring
- ☐ Different for bride and groom
- ☐ Same for bride and groom

☐ Set ring budget

Total $ _____
(You $ _____ Your fiancé $ _____)

☐ Ring sizes
Yours _____ Your fiancé's _____

☐ Choose inscriptions to be engraved

Bride _____

Groom _____

☐ Choose a jeweler

Store _____

Contact _____

Website _____

Address _____

Phone _____

Referred by _____

Notes _____

_____

☐ Order your rings

Date ordered _____ / _____ / _____
Deposit $ _____

Date ready _____ / _____ / _____
Balance $ _____

☐ Review inscriptions before you leave the store.

your marriage license

☐ Find the marriage license bureau in the city or town where you will marry. (Search for the city clerk's office contact info online.)

Website _____

Phone _____

☐ Call the marriage license bureau to confirm

Address _____

Hours _____

Best time to come _____

Do you need blood tests to marry?

Yes _____ No _____

When must you apply?

Within _____ weeks of wedding

Which of the following must you bring with you?

☐ Certified copies of your birth certificates

☐ Proof of citizenship

☐ Government-issued photo ID (driver's license or passport)

☐ Blood test results (if required)

☐ Parental consent (if underage)

☐ Death certificate (if widowed)

☐ Divorce decree (if divorced)

☐ How much will the license cost? $ _____

☐ Payment options?
   ☐ Check
   ☐ Credit card
   ☐ Cash

☐ Make appointments to get blood tests (if required)

Where _____

Address _____

Contact _____

Date   /   /   Time _____

Cost $ _____

☐ Payment options?
   ☐ Check
   ☐ Credit card
   ☐ Cash

Pick up test results _____

Date   /   / _____

☐ Go in person (both of you) to apply for your license. Exactly when you go depends on the window of time (around your wedding date) that a license is valid in your state; it will probably be two or three weeks before, but be sure to research the requirements two months ahead of time to be sure you know what's necessary.

☐ Give your marriage license to your officiant prior to or on your wedding day. He will sign it and file it with the proper office. A copy will be sent to you in a couple of weeks.

☐ File your marriage license in a safe place.

ceremony

ceremony etiquette

We're gay and not sure how the ceremony is going to look—any suggestions?

Your ceremony itself is a binding ritual so make it truly personal. Use the basic outline of a traditional wedding as a starting point, and personalize it from there. The basic components include

The greeting/call to attention: Your officiant tells guests they're here to support the commitment and love between the two of you, and may say a few words about you and your relationship

Declaration of intent/vows: Writing your own vows is a great way to celebrate your commitment to each other—and its uniqueness. You can draw what you like from traditional religious or secular vows; adapt wordings from poems, songs, and prose; or start from scratch and express your feelings in your own words.

Ring exchange: Perhaps you've already given each other rings, and maybe now you'll add bands to go with them or re-enact the ring exchange with a few special words. You may choose not to wear your rings on your left hands, which might suggest that you're married the "traditional" way. Many gay and lesbian couples wear commitment rings on their right hands. You may also choose a nontraditional design and wear it on the traditional finger.

Readings/joining rituals: You don't necessarily have to address gay issues in your readings; you could read about love, friendship, companionship, trust, growth, or whatever tickles your fancy. Joining rituals like a unity candle (the two of you light a mutual candle with flames from two individual candles) or Native American sand blending are perfect ways to symbolize your union.

Pronouncement of marriage and the kiss: This part speaks for itself!

If you choose a religious officiant or another person affiliated with a group (such as an Ethical Humanist), he or she may give you "sample" ceremony wording from which to work. The more secular the officiant, the more creative license you will likely have over what is said, read, sung, or played during the ceremony.

We are of different faiths. What do we do about an officiant?

An interfaith ceremony may take a bit more planning. Be forewarned: One of you may be asked to convert or be baptized, so get the details as soon as possible. The best way to blend the traditions of your faiths is to choose co-officiants. Officiants of most Christian denominations are supportive of interfaith marriage, and more and more Reform rabbis are willing to co-officiate as well (Orthodox or Conservative rabbis may decline). If you can't find two officiants, look for one who's open to including traditions from both religions in the ceremony. Another option is to have a secular ceremony now and then renew your vows in your church or temple and/or your fiancé's church or temple later.

transportation

Your wedding day transportation is more than just a way for you to get from point A to point B; it's an opportunity to make a statement. There are two considerations in the transportation category: luxuries (such as limos for you and your families) and essentials (for example, parking). If you have some extra room in your budget for special wheels, go for something classic, fun, or cool—your arrival can set the tone for the occasion. Try to make transportation arrangements two months before the wedding.

ceremony

wedding transportation worksheet

bride and groom arrival and departure style

- ☐ Stretch limo
- ☐ Town car
- ☐ Classic/vintage car
- ☐ Other _____

- ☐ Luxury car
- ☐ Horse and carriage
- ☐ Your own car

attendants and family transportation

- ☐ Stretch limos (10–12 passengers) # _____
- ☐ Limos (6 passengers) # _____

- ☐ Town cars (4–6 passengers) # _____
- ☐ Their own cars
- ☐ Other _____

guest needs

- ☐ Buses (52 passengers) # _____
- ☐ Vans (7 passengers) # _____
- ☐ Parking attendants (you hire) # _____
- ☐ Valet parking costs (you prepay) $ _____

transportation budget $ _____

wedding weekend transportation worksheet

Decide who needs a ride and when, and then keep track of it here.

WHO'S RIDING?	CAR/COMPANY	PICKUP LOCATION	TIME

finding a car or limo company

To find limousine or other transportation companies, go to **TheKnot.com/limos.**
Make appointments with several car companies.

company name _____

contact person _____

website _____

phone _____

address _____

referred by _____

app't date ____ / ____ / ____   time _____

price estimate $ _____

notes _____

_____

company name _____

contact person _____

website _____

phone _____

address _____

referred by _____

app't date ____ / ____ / ____   time _____

price estimate $ _____

notes _____

_____

questions to ask
limo and car companies

What car types, sizes, and colors are available? How many people can comfortably fit into one?

_____

_____

What about amenities—TV, bar, sunroof?

_____

_____

Is there a special wedding package? (If the company specializes in weddings, you may get perks such as balloons or champagne flutes.)

_____

_____

Is the company a member of the National Limousine Association (or another professional association if you're renting a trolley or buses)?

_____

_____

If you contract for multiple cars, can you get a group discount?

_____

_____

Are you responsible for the cost of gas or mileage, or do the cars come with a set amount of free miles and gas?

_____

_____

What does the driver wear? (It may or may not matter to you whether it's formal clothing, but you should still ask so he doesn't show up in jeans.)

_____

_____

Can you see a copy of the operating license and insurance certificate?

_____

_____

top transportation tips

1 price it out
You'll probably be charged by the hour (starting at $75 per hour for a limousine), and there may be a minimum amount of time you need to contract the cars for.

2 bring the paparazzi
Have your photographer ride with you. Those in-car shots are a total classic.

3 don't make them wait
You may be able to arrange for just pickup or drop-off service, so drivers won't be sitting around (and getting paid) during the ceremony and reception.

4 beware prom time
If your wedding falls during the holidays or graduation season, you may want to book five or six months before your wedding date.

5 give directions
Prepare a call sheet with every name, pickup and drop-off address and time, and detailed directions. Also include an emergency contact number in case the driver gets lost.

ASK CARLEY
transportation

Who's supposed to ride with whom if we hire limousines?

It's really up to you. You can go all out and arrange for a limo to get the guys (groomsmen and groom) to the ceremony site, one for the bridesmaids to get from the bride's home (or hotel suite) to the wedding, and one for the bride and her escort. Or, if it's possible for the wedding party to get to and from the wedding locations in their own cars (or by carpooling together or with guests), you might hire just one limousine for the bride and her escort to ride in to the ceremony site and then to take the newlyweds to the reception. Sometimes the best man and maid of honor share the ride to the reception with the bride and groom.

ceremony

transportation contact cheat sheet

company name _____

contact/point person _____

_____

website _____

address _____

_____

phone _____

e-mail _____

estimate $ _____

deposit $ _____ date paid _____

balance $ _____ date due _____

notes _____

_____

_____

_____

_____

_____

TO-DO CHECKLIST
hiring the car company

☐ Book a limousine or other transportation company by phone. E-mail/fax to confirm; include your wedding date.

☐ Finalize decisions as to

　☐ Limos or cars # _____

　☐ Style and color of each _____

　☐ Additional amenities _____

　☐ Wedding package price $ _____

☐ Request a contract and review for the following critical points:

　☐ Name and contact information for you and the vendor

　☐ Date, times, and locations of pickup and drop-off points (your home, the ceremony site, the reception site, hotels, other places)

☐ Type and number of limousines/cars rented

☐ Amenities supplied with each

☐ Exact hours cars will be hired for

☐ If possible, name(s) of driver(s)

☐ Total cost, including mileage and gas

☐ Overtime fees

☐ Deposit amount due

☐ Balance and date due

☐ Cancellation and refund policy

☐ Company representative's signature

☐ Sign the final contract.

17 photography

If you're going to splurge on anything for your wedding, it should be the pictures. They'll preserve your memories better than anything else you buy. And because the photographer you choose is going to capture your day minute by minute, you'll want to feel comfortable with this person. Rapport is important with all wedding professionals, but it's crucial here!

your wedding photos worksheet

styles you like

☐ Photojournalistic (events captured as they happen)

☐ Candid (similar to photojournalistic with more attention to styling)

☐ Formal portraiture (traditional posed shots)

☐ Creative portraiture (posed in untraditional backdrops)

☐ Black-and-white

☐ Color

☐ Fine-art (shot on film or made to look like it with the right digital camera lens)

☐ Romantic, vintage (filters are applied in postproduction for a glowy look)

☐ Glam (filters are applied in postproduction to get supersaturated colors, as in a fashion magazine)

☐ Edgy, bold (tilted angles and framing)

☐ Quirky (altered colors in postproduction and surprising angles)

subjects to be covered

☐ Prewedding preparations
   ☐ Getting-ready photos

☐ Couple portraits
   ☐ Before the wedding
   ☐ After the ceremony (if you don't
      want to see each other beforehand)

☐ Bridal party portraits
   ☐ All together
   ☐ Individually

☐ Family portraits
   ☐ Immediate family only
   ☐ Extended family

☐ Ceremony

☐ Reception

☐ Other _____

_____

_____

_____

_____

the knot TIP
Find a list of fifty must-have photos for your photo album at **TheKnot.com/50photos.**

additional coverage

☐ Engagement session   ☐ Photo booth

☐ Rehearsal dinner coverage   ☐ Boudoir session

☐ Full wedding weekend coverage   ☐ Other

of wedding album(s) _____

wedding album style

☐ Coffee-table book

☐ Fine-art-style book (prints are mounted on pages)

album features

☐ Matte paper   ☐ Satin paper   ☐ Glossy paper (vision art)

☐ Leather   ☐ Linen   ☐ Silk   ☐ Photo wrap or plain with stamping

☐ Custom embossing on the cover or the binding with your names and wedding date

☐ Image mounted on the front of the cover

☐ Dust jacket around the front (nice coffee-table art-book look)

☐ Presentation box (for the album to sit inside of and to protect it)

beyond the album

☐ Loose prints for framing (usually order print packages)

☐ Canvas prints (photos printed on canvas and then mounted for display)

photo albums

☐ Your photo album   ☐ Parent albums (usually smaller size, such as 10x10 or smaller)

☐ Mini books (copies of your album as giveaways, usually 4x4)

☐ More than one album (one for your engagement photos, another for the wedding)

photography budget $ _____

notes _____

_____

_____

top wedding photo tips

1 trust your photographer
Trust your photographer to keep you on schedule, to frame the shots, and to know what will look best—remember, that's why you hired her!

2 see an actual album
Look at lots of pictures online from previous weddings the photographer has shot to see if he connected to the couple and really captured their day. If possible, also ask to see an unedited gallery—the shots the photographer took before the couple chose the ones they wanted. (This is the photographer's work in the raw.)

3 let guests in on it
If you order prints for family and friends, be sure everyone knows the price per print—or prepare to tack on additional fees to your final tab! Order parents' and guests' albums and prints at the same time as your own to avoid reorder fees.

4 album options
Photographers' albums can be expensive. Make sure to ask who designs the layout (you, her, a combination), how many pages will be included in your album, and whether you can choose how many images go on a page.

5 get behind the scenes
Choose a photo pro you feel extremely comfortable about inviting backstage. Some of the most beautiful wedding moments are those that happen while the bride is dressing, while the family is waiting, or when the couple steals away for a kiss.

6 ignore the camera
When you're taking your portraits, focus on each other rather than on the camera. Whisper an inside joke to one another, remind each other how far you've come since your first date, or recall how you felt the first time he told you he loved you. These will leave you with much more natural expressions than simply saying "cheese."

7 consider a photo booth
It's going to be virtually impossible to get a photo with every guest—or even to guarantee that your photographer will—so renting a photo booth is the perfect solution. Guests can let their personalities shine, especially if you set up a visually interesting backdrop and provide quirky props (funny hats, fake mustaches, mini chalkboards for writing funny messages). The result is guaranteed to make a great addition to your guest book or wedding album.

8 schedule a day-before or day-after shoot
Okay, it's not as essential as, say, engagement photos, but it's a great idea if you're worried about seeing enough of your guests. Instead of taking time the morning of or during cocktail hour, schedule a session for the next day—or even a week after—to snap some couple shots. Yep, you read that right: Get back in the wedding dress (when you're bound to be calmer) and shoot the fun stuff so that you're not bogged down by it on the day of. Do it this way and you'll also give your photographer time to shoot the candid moments of the day.

9 cover your bases . . .
Don't get carried away, but providing your photographer with a top-five list of poses or moments you want is a good way to guarantee you get the photos you're hoping for. Bring in examples that you find online, or point out samples that they've already taken at other weddings. A couple must-haves that we love? The just-after-the-recessional shot (when you're alone and married for the first time!), Mom and Dad at the ceremony (looking proud), and a large overall shot of your reception (to capture the feeling of the evening) are all good ideas.

10 . . . but don't sweat the little things
While it's totally fine to show your photographer the types of shots you like, it's even more important that you're flexible the day of. So if it rains and you can't get that sunny shot of you in a field, grab big umbrellas and a pair of bright-yellow rain boots, and trust your photographer to find the right shot. Same goes for your schedule: If you're stuck in traffic between the ceremony and reception and don't have time to hit up all your favorite city sites with your wedding party, pick a few favorites and move on.

Mary Kate & Ryan
CITY SOPHISTICATES
JULY 23
CHICAGO, IL

Everything from the reception site (the Chicago Cultural Center) to the escort cards (shaped like "L" trains) showcased Mary Kate and Ryan's love of Chicago. Their photographer took it a step further and scouted out the perfect spot for their photo shoot—right in front of the iconic Chicago Avenue "L" station. The overall look of their wedding photos? An homage to their favorite city.

finding your photographer

To find photographers, ask friends with fantastic wedding pictures or get recommendations from your venue or consultant. Check out **TheKnot.com/photographers** to find local photographers (you can also look at their work for the many real weddings featured there). Make appointments with several photographers.

name/company	name/company
website	website
phone	phone
e-mail	e-mail
address	address
referred by	referred by
app't date / / time	app't date / / time
price estimate $	price estimate $
notes	notes

ASK CARLEY
photography

We're on a really tight budget. How smart is it to hire a photography student or ask a guest who's an amateur photographer to take pictures?

Honestly, you'll do better trying to save elsewhere. Even if you find a truly talented student, or if you've always admired your cousin's skill as a shutterbug, keep in mind that if the person doesn't have wedding experience, you probably won't get the results you want. Also, just because someone takes incredible photos doesn't mean they're equipped to capture such a multifaceted event. Our advice: Hire a professional!

questions to ask photographers

What's the photographer's primary style—traditional or photojournalistic? Many are truly good at both.

_____

What is the photographer's philosophy about shooting weddings? (This will give you an idea of the person's expertise and passion.)

_____

_____

How independent is the photographer? Does she prefer that you describe exactly what you want, or would she rather be given free rein to capture the festivities in the way she sees fit?

_____

_____

Will the photographer you talk to be the one taking the pictures at your wedding? (This is crucial! Each photographer's style is his own.)

_____

_____

Will the photographer be shooting any other weddings on your wedding day? (Make sure there are no time constraints.)

_____

_____

Is the photographer open to a list of must-take photos?

_____

_____

How does the photographer determine price? Is it a flat fee or based on the number and kind of prints you think you'll want, the number of hours the photographer works your wedding, the amount of editing time, or a combination?

_____

_____

How will you first be shown photos? (Usually it's an online gallery of proofs through his website.)

_____

_____

What exactly is included in the fee?

_____

_____

How many hours of coverage do you get?

_____

Does the fee include an engagement shoot or any other additional coverage?

_____

Will there be a second shooter?

_____

Does the fee include prints or an album?

_____

Will the photos be retouched?

_____

(CONTINUES)

How long before you'll see the photos? (Most will say they'll send them to you anywhere from four to six weeks after the wedding.)

_____

How does the photographer coordinate with the videographer?

_____

_____

When is the final payment due?

_____

How much extra would it be to have the photographer cover the rehearsal dinner?

_____

_____

Does the photographer do photo booths? Any other fun shoot ideas?

_____

_____

ASK CARLEY
photography

When should formal photos be taken?
The biggest benefit to taking photos before the ceremony is that you will have plenty of time (your photographer will love you). You'll also have fresh hair and makeup! The con is that you'll have to see each other before the ceremony.

(Tip: Stage a "first look" session to get the same shots!) If you're a total traditionalist, you'll want to take photos after the ceremony, but keep in mind that you may have to miss part or all of your cocktail hour in order to get the shots you want.

photographer contact cheat sheet

photographer name(s)/company
_____

website
_____

phone
_____

e-mail
_____

address
_____

details of photography package
_____

_____

_____

estimate $ _____

deposit $ _____   date paid _____

total cost $ _____

balance $ _____   date due _____

notes
_____

_____

_____

_____

ASK CARLEY
photography

How do I stop guests from standing in front of photographers at the ceremony? I don't want any blocked photos!

This is a very good point! Your best bet is to include a note in the ceremony program asking guests to be aware of the photographers there capturing your event. It can be something as simple as "We ask that you remain seated during the ceremony to allow our photographers room to capture the memories."

hiring your photographer

- ☐ Carefully examine samples of each photographer's past work (their "book"). Be sure you're looking at work they shot, not that of other professionals who work at the same studio.

- ☐ Notice whether
  - ☐ Photos are framed well
  - ☐ Photos are over- or underexposed
  - ☐ Details are visible
  - ☐ People look comfortable and relaxed

- ☐ Call references and ask
  - ☐ Did the photographer get the shots they expected and wanted?
  - ☐ Were they satisfied overall?

- ☐ Book your favorite photographer by phone; send an e-mail to confirm and leave a paper trail.

- ☐ Finalize decisions as to
  - ☐ The specific package you're purchasing (if applicable) _____
  - ☐ How many images you'll have to choose from in your online gallery _____
  - ☐ How much time will be needed the day of for posed, formal portraits _____

- ☐ Request a contract and review it for the following critical points:
  - ☐ Name and contact information for you and the vendor
  - ☐ Date, exact times (number of hours), and locations (home, ceremony, reception) where the photographer will work on the wedding day
  - ☐ Name of the photographer(s) who will be shooting your wedding and the number and names of assistants
  - ☐ Package details if you opt for one, like engagement sessions and bridal portraits (you may modify this information later)
  - ☐ The date your online proof gallery will be ready and how long it will be available
  - ☐ When you'll receive your order (albums, prints) once you place it
  - ☐ Length of time the photographer will keep your photo files (or negatives)
  - ☐ Total cost (itemized if possible)
  - ☐ Overtime fees, if applicable
  - ☐ Reorder price, if you should decide to order additional pictures later
  - ☐ Deposit amount due
  - ☐ Balance and date due
  - ☐ Cancellation and refund policy
  - ☐ Photographer's signature

- ☐ Sign the final contract.

18

videography

We can't tell you how many times couples have said that their wedding was over before they knew it, and they feel like they missed a lot of what went on. A wedding video is the best way to capture the experience from the day. Since photographers and videographers work together quite closely, you'll probably want to hire these professionals at about the same time; you may even want to ask your photographer (whom you should hire first) for a referral.

wedding videography worksheet

wedding video style

- ☐ Documentary   ☐ Hollywood
- ☐ Stylized (Super 8 or 16 mm for a vintage look)
- ☐ Mixed media (a mix of film and digital)

elements to be filmed/footage to be included

- ☐ Prewedding preparations (getting makeup done, putting on your dress)
- ☐ Ceremony (vows, ring exchange, kiss)
- ☐ Rehearsal dinner/welcome party
- ☐ Reception
- ☐ Couple interview   ☐ Guest interviews
- ☐ Music video (an edited mix of guests singing along to your favorite song)
- ☐ Guest video booth

what you want included in your video package

- ☐ Full-feature video (20–30 minutes)
- ☐ Highlights video (5–10 minutes)
- ☐ Trailer video (1–3 minutes, usually delivered within a month of the wedding)
- ☐ Same-day edit (a short highlights video created on-site to show at the reception)
- ☐ Full footage of speeches and toasts (unedited)

special considerations

_____

_____

videography budget $ _____

ASK CARLEY
videography

What should a good videographer include for the price of a package?

Whether you choose bare-bones coverage or all the bells and whistles, any videographer should supply the following: backup camera(s), lights, batteries, wireless microphones (if you want them used)—and courtesy to guests. You can also expect interesting shots and creative and entertaining coverage of your day. One of the most important reasons for hiring a professional to record your wedding, besides his expertise, is the ability to edit a video smoothly. Every package should include at least one edited tape.

top wedding video tips

1 do your homework

Set aside a couple hours to research videographers. And don't just watch highlight reels. Take the time to watch through entire full-length films to get a feel for the way he or she tells the story of the wedding.

2 ways to save

Consider having only the ceremony filmed. Forgo complicated editing (but you'll want at least minimal editing to make the video more watchable—otherwise, you'll end up with four to eight hours of loose video, some of which is not so interesting). Opt for a single camera. Forget shooting on film (digital is cheaper).

3 keep it short

No one (except maybe your mom) wants to spend four hours watching your wedding video. Keep the edited film around thirty minutes. Also, try to get an even shorter, ten-minute version—a "highlights" reel to show the rest of your friends and family.

4 double coverage

If you hire your photographer and videographer separately, ask that they meet before the wedding to coordinate shooting styles and strategies. If they've worked together before, that can be a bonus. But don't assume that their quality will be the same; interview each professional separately. If you're pressured to hire them as a team and it makes you uncomfortable, look elsewhere.

5 be heard

Discuss where and how you'll be mic'd for the ceremony; also make sure it's okay with your officiant. Without mics, you won't hear the vows or those memorable toasts from friends and family.

ASK CARLEY
videography

If we already have a photographer, do we really need a videographer too?

It's up to you. A photographer usually comes first, but video has a completely different feel. Because it's in real time and in living color—and you can include pictures from your pasts and music that's important to you, and guest interviews—a video is a very full and emotional way to preserve your wedding memories. Honestly, not having a video is one of couples' most common regrets.

finding your videographer

Your photographer, planner, and site manager are your best sources for finding good videographers. Also, ask recently married friends who had good experiences and whose videos you've seen and liked. There are listings of local videographers at **TheKnot.com/video.** Make appointments with several videographers.

name/company _____

website _____

phone _____

e-mail _____

address _____

referred by _____

app't date ___ / ___ / ___ time _____

price estimate $ _____

notes _____

_____

name/company _____

website _____

phone _____

e-mail _____

address _____

referred by _____

app't date ___ / ___ / ___ time _____

price estimate $ _____

notes _____

_____

ASK CARLEY
videography

Are certain venues more conducive than others to videography?

Weddings not held in a house of worship are often better for videography. Outdoor weddings, in a park or backyard, can give the cameraperson more freedom. Weddings held in a banquet hall or hotel allow the videographer to set up in the best locations and get the shots the bride and groom want. Basically, the less traditional the setting for the wedding, the more liberty the videographer has.

questions to ask videographers

What's the videographer's style—artsy, documentary, or cinematic? Does this work with what you want?

_____

_____

Has the videographer done many weddings? What's his approach when it comes to filming a wedding? (This clues you in to his experience and philosophy.)

_____

_____

Has the videographer worked with your photographer before? How does the videographer coordinate with a wedding photographer? (This is really important!)

_____

_____

Has this person ever shot a wedding at your ceremony and/or reception site? If so, can you see that video?

_____

_____

How many other weddings is the videographer doing on your wedding day or weekend? (Make sure there are no time constraints.)

_____

_____

Will the videographer you're speaking to be the one who will shoot your wedding?

_____

_____

What kind and how many cameras and microphones will the videographer use? (Sound is a huge differentiator in quality.)

_____

_____

How does the crew stay unobtrusive during the ceremony and key moments? (Are there extra lights? Are they subtle or obvious?)

_____

_____

How does the videographer charge? Are there packages? Ask for a price list.

_____

_____

notes

_____

_____

_____

_____

_____

videographer contact cheat sheet

name(s)/company _____

website _____

phone _____

e-mail _____

address _____

_____

details of videography package _____

_____

estimate $ _____

deposit $ _____ date paid _____

total cost $ _____

balance $ _____ date due _____

TO-DO CHECKLIST

hiring your videographer

- ☐ Watch samples. Notice whether:
  - ☐ The images are clear (not out of focus)
  - ☐ The lighting is right (not too dim)
  - ☐ The sound quality is good
  - ☐ The editing is smooth
  - ☐ If special effects were added (vintage 8 mm effects, for example), they look professional
- ☐ Call references and ask about their videos.
- ☐ Book your favorite videographer, and send an e-mail to confirm and leave a paper trail.
- ☐ Finalize decisions as to
  - ☐ What (ceremony, reception, or both) will be filmed _____
  - ☐ The components of the package you're purchasing (if applicable) _____
  - ☐ Special requests (people and events your videographer should capture; songs to use in editing) _____

- ☐ Request a contract and review for the following critical points:
  - ☐ Name and contact information
  - ☐ Date, exact times (number of hours), and locations (home, ceremony, reception)
  - ☐ Name of the videographer(s) as well as the number of assistants
  - ☐ Number and kind(s) of cameras to be used
  - ☐ Number of DVDs you'll receive, and complete package details
  - ☐ Date when your unedited video will be ready
  - ☐ Date when your finished video will be ready
  - ☐ Total cost, with all charges itemized
  - ☐ Overtime fee, if applicable
  - ☐ Reorder prices
  - ☐ Deposit amount due
  - ☐ Balance and date due
  - ☐ Cancellation and refund policy
  - ☐ Videographer's signature
- ☐ Sign the final contract.

19

entertainment

The music can make (or break!) your reception. Whether you hire a sixteen-piece swing band or a skilled DJ, great music sets the mood for the day, so choose carefully. The first decision is band vs. DJ, and that will largely be determined by your budget. Once you've settled that, get started on your search; as always, the best professionals get booked unbelievably early.

your reception music worksheet

cocktail-hour music

☐ DJ

☐ Big band (swing)

☐ Jazz group (saxophone, bass, drum, vocals)

☐ International music (steel drum, mariachi band)

☐ Classical (piano or piano and vocal)

☐ Bluegrass/country band

Specific songs you may want to consider/include

_____

_____

_____

_____

_____

_____

_____

_____

_____

_____

_____

Hours of music needed _____

cocktail-hour music budget $ _____

reception music (check all that you want)

☐ DJ

☐ Big band (swing)

☐ Jazz group (saxophone, bass, drum, vocals)

☐ International music (steel drum, mariachi band)

☐ Classical (piano or piano and vocal)

☐ Bluegrass/country band

☐ Funk band

☐ R & B band

☐ Cover band

Specific songs you may want to consider/include

_____

_____

_____

_____

Traditional dances

_____

_____

_____

_____

Hours of reception music needed _____

reception music budget $ _____

the knot TIP
Find thousands of song ideas at
TheKnot.com/weddingsongs.

top reception music planning tips

1 think of your guests

Maybe you love indie alt rock music, but what about Grandma and Grandpa? Be sure the band or DJ can play some Sinatra and Cole Porter standards, too.

2 size it up

Consider the size of your reception room and your crowd. An intimate space is not going to fit Jerry Jones & His Orchestra. A three-piece combo may not cut it for a guest list of four hundred. A good rule of thumb: at least a six-piece band for groups of a hundred people or more.

3 make sure you have an emcee

If you want the bandleader or DJ to announce the wedding party and the events of the reception, be sure he has the necessary information. Write down all names (with pronunciations), their roles, and their relation to you (mother, best friend, and so on). More important, if you don't want the entertainment to make announcements, be sure they know that, too. (Do remember that you will need someone to announce when you want your guests to head to the buffet, but that can be done table by table by your banquet manager.)

ASK CARLEY
cocktail-hour music

What do we do for cocktail-hour music?

Cocktail hours need their own ambience and are often a good place to be more unique or eclectic musically. Unique options are a jazz band, a pianist and vocalist duo (à la Sinatra), or a steel-drum, bluegrass, or mariachi band. Also consider asking whether a few of the reception band members are available to be your jazz combo or quartet during cocktails. You'll just tack the extra fee onto what you're already paying, as opposed to contracting with a whole new group. Do make sure they're going to sound different, not just like a smaller version of the band your guests will hear later.

finding your
reception band or dj

To find reception bands or DJs, go to **TheKnot.com/music** to see listings and hear performers, check local wedding magazines, see local gigs in clubs or at other people's weddings or other special events, and definitely ask recently married friends for recommendations. Nothing is better than a referral from someone who's seen the performers live. Make appointments with several bands or DJs.

dj/band name _____

website _____

e-mail _____

phone _____

referred by _____

app't date ___ / ___ / ___ time ___

type of music _____

price estimate $ _____

notes _____

_____

dj/band name _____

website _____

e-mail _____

phone _____

referred by _____

app't date ___ / ___ / ___ time ___

type of music _____

price estimate $ _____

notes _____

_____

ASK CARLEY
reception music

How do we choose between a band and a DJ?
Beyond budget, there are three factors: (1) authenticity—with a DJ, the songs you hear will be the original versions you're familiar with, whereas a band will play their own interpretations; (2) the action factor—live entertainment has a different feel than recorded music; and (3) space considerations.

questions to ask
reception bands & djs

What's the band's signature sound? Are they a jazz band, rock band, "wedding band" (as in they specialize in playing at weddings)? Find out what type of music they consider their forte.

_____

_____

Does the DJ specialize in a certain type of music—Top 40, swing, jazz, country—or do they offer a variety of genres? Can you see a sample playlist? Can you listen to one?

_____

_____

Is the band or DJ willing to mix it up a bit (play some standards in addition to their typical rock fare, for example)? Will they perform or play traditional standards, such as the hora or tarantella, if requested?

_____

_____

How does the DJ or band feel about a request list? (The answer should be along the lines of "We'll try to honor your requests, but we also need to go with the flow to see what works well.")

_____

_____

How many band members are available? If you're interviewing a DJ, does he or she work with a partner, an assistant, or dancers?

_____

_____

If there's a song you want played and the band isn't familiar with it, are they willing to learn it in time for your wedding? Will you need to supply the sheet music? If it's a DJ, can you lend your own iPod, or are they willing to buy what you'd like played?

_____

_____

Does the band or DJ bring equipment (amps, mics, and so on), or would you and/or your reception site need to supply it?

_____

_____

How much room will the band or DJ need? Will the DJ need a table to set up on?

_____

_____

How much time before the reception would the band or DJ need to set up?

_____

_____

Is there a minimum amount of time the band or DJ will play?

_____

_____

(CONTINUES)

How many breaks does the band or DJ typically take? Will they break in rotation, so someone is always playing? Or will they play taped music during breaks?

_____

_____

What will the band or DJ wear?

_____

_____

How much does the band or DJ charge for a four- or five-hour reception? If there's a range, what accounts for the difference between the high and low prices?

_____

_____

What is the overtime policy? Is the charge per hour or half hour?

_____

_____

Ask yourself: Does the band or DJ seem flexible and willing to play the music you want? (It's good to give them some freedom, but if you sense that they're resistant to your desires, reconsider.)

_____

_____

ASK CARLEY

cocktail-hour music

How do we ensure that none of those cheesy wedding songs like "YMCA" and "Shout" are played at our wedding?

If there's something you don't want played, let your DJ or band know. It's really that simple. Why would you sacrifice the mood of this important day just so your friends and relatives can do the chicken dance? Line dances can be fun for a child's Communion or bar mitzvah, but if you want your wedding to really reflect your tastes, you can skip the tribute to the Village People. When you're creating your list of must-play songs for your band or DJ, you should feel free to include a separate section for your "under no circumstances shall these be played" picks. If you've already got the right mix of music keeping your guests on the floor, chances are no one will even notice you've skipped the silly songs.

reception music contact cheat sheet

cocktail-hour musicians

musician name(s)/company _____

website _____

phone _____

e-mail _____

address _____

_____

estimate $ _____

deposit $ _____ date paid _____

total cost $ _____

balance $ _____ date due _____

notes _____

_____

_____

_____

_____

_____

_____

_____

_____

_____

reception musicians/dj

musician name(s)/company _____

website _____

phone _____

e-mail _____

address _____

_____

estimate $ _____

deposit $ _____ date paid _____

total cost $ _____

balance $ _____ date due _____

notes _____

_____

_____

_____

_____

_____

_____

_____

_____

_____

hiring your reception band or dj

- ☐ Ask to listen to a demo of each band's live music, or to watch a video of a DJ performing (but don't make your decision based solely on their demos). Ask if it's possible to see each band or DJ in action (you may be able to poke your head into another reception).

- ☐ When you see each band or DJ perform, notice
  - ☐ Stage presence/voice
  - ☐ Interaction with the crowd
  - ☐ Whether the music is continuous and/or has smooth transitions
  - ☐ If the band or DJ seems comfortable/in control

- ☐ Call references and ask:
  - ☐ Did the crowd enjoy themselves? Did people dance?
  - ☐ Did the band or DJ play most of the songs on the couple's playlist?
  - ☐ Did the expected musicians show up at the event?

- ☐ Book your favorite band or DJ. E-mail or request a confirmation to ensure a paper trail.

- ☐ Finalize decisions such as
  - ☐ If it's a band, how many musicians and what instruments
  - ☐ Music to be sung or played:
    First dance _____
    Father-daughter dance _____
    Mother-son dance _____
    Traditional songs _____
    Last dance _____

Must-play songs _____

_____

_____

- ☐ Request a contract and review it for the following critical points:
  - ☐ Name and contact information for you and the vendor
  - ☐ Your wedding date, address of location, and band's/DJ's exact arrival time
  - ☐ Whether the bandleader or DJ will also serve as emcee
  - ☐ The number of hours the band or DJ will work
  - ☐ Any equipment you or the site needs to supply—chairs, tables, music stands, amplifiers
  - ☐ Equipment the band or DJ will supply
  - ☐ Must-play songs (or date by which you need to supply song list)
  - ☐ Any songs you definitely don't want played
  - ☐ Any agreements for you to supply music off your iPod or sheet music
  - ☐ What the band or DJ will wear
  - ☐ Total cost
  - ☐ Overtime rate if your reception runs long
  - ☐ Deposit amount due
  - ☐ Balance and date due
  - ☐ Cancellation and refund policy
  - ☐ Bandleader or DJ's signature

- ☐ Sign the final contract.

20

flowers & décor

How much energy and time you devote to planning your décor depends largely on your ceremony and reception sites: An ornate space will require minimal additions. If flowers and décor aren't critical to you, it's fine to book someone six months before the wedding. On the other hand, if you're working with a clean slate, there will be more work to do. A full-service floral designer should be booked as soon as you've nailed down your wedding location.

your flowers & décor worksheet

floral style

- ☐ Traditional
- ☐ Old-world, ornate
- ☐ Romantic

- ☐ Bold, festive
- ☐ Minimal/modern
- ☐ Whimsical

- ☐ Rustic
- ☐ Beachy

flowers

- ☐ Seasonal flowers
- ☐ Greens (grasses)

- ☐ Exotic flowers
- ☐ Berries and branches

- ☐ Succulents
- ☐ Surprising elements (milk-glass vases, reclaimed wood)

Favorite flowers _____

_____

colors

- ☐ Monochromatic
- ☐ Traditional (white, pastels)

- ☐ Multicolored
- ☐ Modern (dark hues, citrus shades)

- ☐ All-white

Favorite colors _____

_____

décor

- ☐ Aisle runner
- ☐ Fabric draping
- ☐ Lounge furniture

- ☐ Aisle decorations
- ☐ Chair covers

- ☐ Lighting
- ☐ Ceremony arch/huppah

> *the knot* TIP
> See and clip your favorite flower photos
> at **TheKnot.com/flowerphotos.**

floral needs

CEREMONY

☐ Bridal bouquet/tossing bouquet

☐ Bridesmaid bouquets # _____

☐ Flower girl's flowers (or basket of petals)

☐ Corsages for moms and grandmothers # _____

☐ Groom's boutonniere

☐ Boutonnieres for groomsmen, ushers, dads, grandfathers # _____

☐ Altar arrangements # _____

☐ Flower-covered arch or huppah

☐ Rose petals for tossing

PARTIES

☐ Rehearsal dinner arrangements

☐ Welcome party arrangements

RECEPTION

☐ Reception table centerpieces # _____

☐ Reception buffet table flowers

☐ Reception cake table flowers

☐ Additional greenery (such as potted plants)

☐ Door or doorway decorations

☐ Escort card table arrangements

☐ Bar and cocktail-hour arrangements

☐ Bathroom arrangements

☐ Other _____

flower & décor budget $ _____

Tracy & Matt
HISTORIC ELEGANCE
JULY 23
NEW YORK, NY

An "old New York" theme offered a sense of drama for Tracy and Matt's day—and fit their historic ballroom setting. Their florist doused the space with white phalaenopsis orchid candelabra centerpieces and then fashioned an all-white bridal bouquet out of Casablanca lilies, calla lilies, and more orchids for a timeless look.

top flowers & décor tips

1 find your match
When you're researching florists, make sure your style matches theirs. Some florists specialize in tall, lush, ornate centerpieces, while others are better at modern minimalist arrangements. If a florist can't show you work that matches the aesthetic you're after, keep looking.

2 stay in season and go local
Easily acquired flowers will probably be less expensive. Choose built-in décor—if your reception site is a garden or is otherwise very ornate, you can use fewer flowers and still have a stunning space.

3 mind your holidays
A church will already be beautifully decorated for Christmas or Easter. On the other hand, roses (and florists) are in major demand (read: expensive) around Valentine's Day and Mother's Day. If your wedding is close to a flower-heavy holiday, focus on reception centerpieces and the bridal bouquet.

4 trust your florist
Hire someone you trust to make the right floral decisions—someone who instinctively knows what will look good together. Don't obsess or micromanage—you hire a florist to create beautiful arrangements according to your vision, and that's exactly what your florist will do.

5 show, don't tell
Bring your inspiration boards, a bridesmaid-dress fabric swatch, and/or a photograph of the wedding gown when you first see a florist. Those things will help convey your style.

6 pick a palette
If color is the most important thing to you, just give your florist guidelines and let her choose the most appropriate (and gorgeous) flowers available at the time of your wedding.

7 choose hearty blooms
If your wedding will be in a very humid climate—especially if it's outside—certain flowers will wilt before you say your vows. Ask your florist which ones can withstand your weather.

8 read up on the flower rules
Ask your officiant if your ceremony site has any restrictions about floral decorations.

9 keep an open mind
Top floral designers are including elements such as succulents, herbs, berries, fruits, and grasses in arrangements. The look is modern, unique, and definitely worth considering!

10 keep your timeline in mind
Coordinate personal-flower delivery times with the arrival of the photographer—you'll want them to be worn or held in formal pictures.

finding your floral designer

To find a great florist, ask for recommendations from newlyweds you know, as well as your caterer, photographer, and wedding consultant (obviously). Check out **TheKnot.com/florists** for local wedding florists, or visit local flower shops to see if you might want to approach them for your wedding. Make appointments with several floral designers.

florist name/company	florist name/company
website	website
e-mail	e-mail
phone	phone
referred by	referred by
app't date / / time	app't date / / time
price estimate $	price estimate $
notes	notes

ASK CARLEY
wedding flowers

How do we decide on flowers for the wedding party? And what about the groom's boutonniere—should it match the bride's bouquet?

The bride's bouquet is definitely the starting point for choosing personal flowers—all the other arrangements should complement hers. The bridesmaid bouquets should echo the color and shape of the bride's but are usually smaller. They should also complement the color of the bridesmaids' dresses.

The groom's boutonniere should be distinct from the groomsmen's somehow, perhaps with an extra bloom in a different color. It's nice if he wears a flower that's in the bride's bouquet as well. (Dads and grandfathers can wear boutonnieres to match the groomsmen.) Flower girls can carry mini bouquets that match the bridesmaids', wear a head wreath of blooms that are in the bride's bouquet, or carry a basket of petals or a pomander (a flower ball suspended on ribbon).

questions to ask
floral designers

Can you see photographs of past work? (Real bouquets and arrangements will give you a better idea than photos—especially photos that aren't of the florist's actual work but show things the florist says he can do.)

_____

_____

Does the florist's style—and the overall look of the shop/studio—match yours? (This is common sense; you should get a good gut feeling.)

_____

_____

Has the florist done weddings at your ceremony and/or reception sites before? (She may have pictures of arrangements done at your site and will be knowledgeable about what sizes, shapes, and colors work in the space.)

_____

_____

If not, will she stop by prior to the wedding to check out the space?

_____

_____

Will the florist simply drop flowers off for your wedding, or will she spend time at the sites setting up and making sure everything is in order? (You'll pay for a full-service florist, but you get what you pay for.)

_____

_____

How big is the shop (that is, the staff), and who will ultimately be working on your wedding? (Make sure it's the floral designer with whom you discuss your vision.)

_____

_____

How many weddings will the florist be doing on the same day or weekend as yours?

_____

_____

Does the florist offer any rental items—vases, potted plants, arches, trellises, candelabras, urns? Or must you get those things from a rental company?

_____

_____

Does the florist act as a designer or stylist? Will he style the entire table, from linens and tableware to chair covers?

_____

_____

What about draping? Does the florist work with someone?

_____

_____

floral designer contact cheat sheet

floral designer name/company _____

website _____

phone _____

e-mail _____

address _____

_____

estimate $ _____

deposit $ _____   date paid _____

total cost $ _____

balance $ _____   date due _____

notes _____

_____

_____

ASK CARLEY
wedding flowers

I want to keep my bouquet—do I have to toss it during the reception?

You don't have to toss the actual bouquet you carry down the aisle if you don't want to—many brides have their florist create a smaller tossing bouquet, to be given away to a lucky female guest. If you don't like the idea of tossing a bouquet to all of your single girlfriends (and risking possibly embarrassing them), you might want to skip the tradition altogether. Give your tossing bouquet to the woman in the room who's been married the longest, or even your grandmother.

hiring your floral designer

☐ Have each florist put together a detailed proposal for your wedding, based on what you've told him about your wedding vision and floral budget. If you've spoken about many different ideas, ask him to offer several options for your table arrangements so that you can choose what works best.

☐ Book your favorite florist. Send her an e-mail confirmation or get it in writing to ensure you have a paper trail.

☐ Finalize flower decisions—types, colors, and amounts:

   ☐ Bouquets (bride) _____

   ☐ Bouquets (bridesmaids) _____

   ☐ Throwaway bouquet for the bouquet toss _____

   ☐ Boutonnieres (groom, groomsmen, dads) _____

   ☐ Corsages (mothers, grandmothers) _____

   ☐ Floral head wreath (flower girl, bride) _____

   ☐ Ceremony arrangements (for around the altar or stage, lining the aisle, door wreaths) _____

   ☐ Huppah decorations _____

   ☐ Petals for guests to toss _____

   ☐ Reception arrangements (centerpieces, extra flowers for the head table, cake or cake-table flowers, arches over doors, any other room arrangements) _____

☐ Request a contract and review it for the following critical points:

   ☐ Name and contact information for you and the vendor

   ☐ Date, times, and locations of your ceremony and reception

   ☐ An itemized list of all the flower arrangements you've chosen, from bouquets to centerpieces, including the specific blooms ("Black Magic roses," etc.). You may modify this later when you've made final decisions.

   ☐ Flower alternatives, should certain blooms be unavailable on your wedding day (also include anything unacceptable to you)

   ☐ A list of anything else the florist will supply: centerpiece vases, a trellis for the ceremony site, other accessories

   ☐ Arrival times and time needed for setup at the ceremony and reception sites

   ☐ Where and when bouquets and boutonnieres should be delivered (home, hotel, site—this information can be supplied at a later date if necessary)

   ☐ The name of the florist who will be on hand before/during setup of the wedding

   ☐ Total cost (itemized if possible)

   ☐ Delivery and setup fees

   ☐ Deposit amount due

   ☐ Balance and date due

   ☐ Cancellation and refund policy

   ☐ Florist's signature

☐ Sign the final contract.

21
day-of details

As you'd expect, the last fourteen days before your wedding can be a total blur! Between your own nervousness and all the seemingly countless details to manage, you might wonder if you're actually going to make it. Here are some cheat sheets to make sure you stay calm and relaxed—and don't get caught in a last-minute panic.

wedding weekend
accommodations & timeline

2 days before

11:00 a.m.	One last walk-through with event planner
1:00 p.m.	Bridesmaid luncheon
4:00 p.m.	Ceremony rehearsal (only if you're having a welcome party the day before)

2 days before   ____ / ____ / ____

_____ _____
_____ _____
_____ _____
_____ _____
_____ _____
_____ _____
_____ _____

day before

4:00 p.m.	Ceremony rehearsal
5:00 p.m.	Rehearsal dinner

day before   ____ / ____ / ____

_____ _____
_____ _____
_____ _____
_____ _____

ACCOMMODATIONS

night-before accommodations

bride _____

groom _____

bride's family _____

_____

groom's family _____

_____

wedding-night accommodations

bride and groom _____

bride's family _____

_____

groom's family _____

_____

wedding day

9:00 a.m.	Bride and bridesmaids meet for hair and makeup (and first person gets hair and makeup done)
11:00 a.m.	Groom and groomsmen meet
12:00 p.m.	Hair and makeup for bride
12:30 p.m.	Serve lunch
2:00 p.m.	"First look" photos
	Wedding party travels to ceremony
3:30 p.m.	Ceremony music begins
4:15 p.m.	Line up (bridal party to arrive no later than 3:50 p.m.)
4:30 p.m.	Ceremony begins
5:30 p.m.	Ceremony ends
5:45 p.m.	Cocktail hour starts (bridal party and close family stay for photos)
6:30 p.m.	Guests head from the cocktail hour into the reception
6:45 p.m.	Emcee begins introducing the wedding party
7:00 p.m.	First dance, followed by parent dances
7:15 p.m.	A blessing and then dinner is served
8:00 p.m.	Cake cutting
8:35 p.m.	Dancing starts (and bouquet toss)
10:00 p.m.	Guests get ready for send-off

wedding day _____/_____/_____

the knot TIP
Find more sample timelines at
TheKnot.com/timelines.

big day & beyond

top last-minute tips

1 delegate
The closer your wedding day gets, the more responsibilities and contact with vendors you should assign to attendants and family.

2 do it now
Bite the bullet and create the seating chart so that you can hand it off to your reception site manager or caterer at least a week before the wedding. Decide where to post the directory (or display of table cards) to inform each guest where to be seated.

3 take notes
Prepare a day-of package for each vendor. Note any last-minute requests you have made on paper. Also include items they will need on the actual day, in case they forget their copies (for example, the song list for the DJ, special food requests for the caterer, a list of must-get people for the photographer).

4 dress up
Several days before your wedding, try on your entire ensemble one last time. Catch any dangling threads or last-minute alterations that are needed on the dress. Confirm the comfort of your underclothes and shoes—don't hesitate to buy replacements if you have any problems.

5 be generous
Don't let your gifts for your wedding party, parents, or each other get left off the list because of lack of time. Last-minute gift ideas include bottles of fine wine, flowers, and gift certificates to favorite restaurants.

6 meet and greet
Leave a nice welcome note at the hotel for each guest who has traveled far to attend your wedding. Have a list ready of who is arriving when and where (including phone number) so that you know when to drop off welcome bags at the hotel.

7 check the weather
If you're marrying in winter or summer, keep potential blizzards and heat waves in mind and plan accordingly (for example, make sure the church parking lot will be shoveled; double-check the air-conditioning at the reception hall).

8 make contact
Create a wedding day contact list. Lucky you—there's one on page 179.

9 call to confirm
When you call each vendor the day before the wedding, make sure to confirm that they have the address and directions to the site, your day-of contact information (cell phone), and confirm the name of their point person during the wedding. If they sound confused about any of the above information, put it in writing for them and e-mail it. (We know we've been through all of this before, but we can't stress enough the importance of this last-minute attention to detail.) Also confirm a wedding-day phone number for them.

10 don't be a perfectionist
Things are bound to go wrong—what you *can* control is how much you let it bother you. Those tend to be some of the most spontaneous moments anyway.

wedding day tipping worksheet

Wedding workers usually get a gratuity if you're happy with their services. Tips are generally given at the end of the wedding; you might want to designate someone to be in charge of handing them over. Before you start liberally giving out cash, however, check the bill—particularly the catering bill—to see if a gratuity is included. And if you're unsure of the tipping policy at your reception site, talk to the manager for suggestions. Put tips in sealed envelopes to be given to your vendors. See the top of page 178 for some tipping guidelines.

vendor	amount ($)	# of workers	total
Ceremony site staff	$ _____	_____	$ _____
Ceremony musicians	$ _____	_____	$ _____
Banquet manager	$ _____	_____	$ _____
Maître d'	$ _____	_____	$ _____
Waitstaff	$ _____	_____	$ _____
Bartenders	$ _____	_____	$ _____
Restroom attendant(s)	$ _____	_____	$ _____
Coatroom attendant(s)	$ _____	_____	$ _____
Valet(s)	$ _____	_____	$ _____
Security guard(s)	$ _____	_____	$ _____
Reception musicians	$ _____	_____	$ _____
Hairstylist	$ _____	_____	$ _____
Makeup artist	$ _____	_____	$ _____
Delivery driver(s)	$ _____	_____	$ _____
Limo driver(s)	$ _____	_____	$ _____

total cash needed $ _____

wedding vendor tipping guide

When calculating the total allotted for each wedding category,
make sure you account for tips.

- **Club or banquet manager:** 15 to 20 percent of the reception bill
- **Maître d' or captain:** 15 to 20 percent of the reception bill
- **Waitstaff:** At least $20 each; maître d' will distribute tips for you
- **Bartenders:** $25 to $40 each
- **Restroom and coatroom attendants:** $1 per guest

- **Valets:** $1 per car, or arrange a gratuity
- **Limo driver(s):** 15 to 20 percent of the total bill (to distribute between them)
- **Delivery driver(s):** $10 each
- **DJ crew or band members:** $20 to $25 each
- **Hairstylist and makeup artist:** 15 to 20 percent of bill
- Have an extra $200 on you ($10 and $20 bills) for unexpected occasions

your day-of emergency bag

Many a bride (and groom) has been grateful that she—or her maid of honor—had
the foresight to bring a last-minute-glitch kit to the ceremony and reception.

- ☐ Your phone
- ☐ Small brush or comb
- ☐ Travel-size hairspray
- ☐ Barrettes, bobby pins, ponytail holder
- ☐ Nail file
- ☐ Safety pins
- ☐ Clear nail polish (for stocking runs)
- ☐ Clear Band-Aids
- ☐ Breath mints
- ☐ Tums, aspirin, ibuprofen

- ☐ Tissues
- ☐ Small mirror
- ☐ Tampons, pads
- ☐ Krazy Glue (for a broken heel or similar small disasters)
- ☐ White masking tape (a quick fix for hems)
- ☐ Static-cling spray
- ☐ Chalk or Ivory soap (to cover unexpected dress stains)
- ☐ Mini bag of pretzels or granola bar

- ☐ Small bottle of water
- ☐ Dental floss
- ☐ Lavender or chamomile oil (to calm you down!)
- ☐ Asthma inhaler or other medication
- ☐ Add your own

  _____

  _____

  _____

  _____

  _____

wedding day contact list

ceremony site

address
_____

_____

_____

phone
_____

reception site

address
_____

_____

_____

phone
_____

family and bridal party

_____
_____
_____
_____
_____
_____
_____
_____
_____
_____
_____
_____
_____
_____
_____
_____
_____
_____

vendors

_____
_____
_____
_____
_____
_____
_____
_____
_____
_____
_____
_____
_____
_____
_____
_____
_____
_____

add your own last-minute reminders

_____

_____

_____

_____

_____

_____

_____

_____

_____

_____

_____

_____

_____

_____

_____

_____

_____

_____

_____

_____

_____

_____

_____

_____

_____

honeymoon

You can start planning your honeymoon as soon as you get engaged, and serious booking of your trip should happen four to five months before your wedding. Start right away if you're planning a foreign excursion, a complicated itinerary that takes you to several destinations, or a trip to a popular island or resort. Bon voyage!

your honeymoon worksheet

So what are the options? Figure out what you really want for your honeymoon.
Try to plan a trip that blends as many of your top priorities as possible.

what you want (check all that apply)

☐ Beach (sun, sand)

☐ City (culture, history, museums)

☐ Sporty (hiking, water sports)

☐ Cozy lodge (skiing, fireplaces)

☐ Exotic adventure (off-the-map spots)

location

☐ Foreign

☐ In nature

☐ Seaside

☐ Domestic

☐ Urban

☐ Combination

accommodations

☐ Deluxe resort

☐ All-inclusive

☐ Boutique hotel

☐ Bed-and-breakfast

☐ Length #_____ days/weeks

departure

☐ Directly from wedding
   (Date _____ / _____/ _____
   Earliest time _____)

☐ Next day/that week
   (Date _____ / _____/ _____
   Earliest time _____)

☐ Later date
   (Date _____ / _____/ _____
   Earliest time _____)

dream destinations

_____

_____

_____

_____

honeymoon budget $ _____

working with a travel agent
or honeymoon planner

A travel agent can do everything from making your airline reservations to reserving theater tickets—saving you time and frustration. He also can help you get the most for your budget by finding great fares, recommending less-expensive alternatives, or selling you seats on a flight his company has chartered (a service offered by some agencies).

name _____	name _____
e-mail _____	e-mail _____
website _____	website _____
phone _____	phone _____
referred by _____	referred by _____
app't date __/__/__ time ___	app't date __/__/__ time ___
notes _____	notes _____

ASK CARLEY
honeymoon

Do I pay for a travel agent?

Most often, the service of a travel agent is free, while some specialists, particularly those who plan high-end luxury honeymoons, get a commission from the hotel or airline, not from you. Contact several travel agents so you can find an agency that specializes in your dream trip—luxury travel, cruising the Caribbean, adventure—and an agent who's flexible and willing to work with you.

big day & beyond

top honeymoon tips

1 know the nitty-gritty

If it's an international trip, ask yourselves the following questions before you book:

- Do we need shots, passports, special visas, or other papers?
- Is there a good taxi or bus system, or will we need a car to get around?
- What's the weather like during the time we plan to go?
- Do we need a converter for our blow-dryer/curling iron/handheld massager?
- How do we get from the airport to the hotel? (Are transfers included?)
- Is it safe? Are there areas to avoid?
- Can we drink the water and/or eat fresh foods?

2 consider the all-inclusive resort option

One flat fee covers your room, plus all meals, unlimited drinks, entertainment, tips, taxes, airport transfers, and a list of activities (most with instruction and equipment). (Cruises do not include soda, alcoholic drinks, or tips.) Off-site excursions, rental cars, and spa treatments are usually not included except as part of a package.

3 special treatment

Come on, splurge a little—it's your honeymoon! Before you book your flight, look into what upgrades are possible. You might be able to request special in-flight meals and drinks.

4 spend a night nearby

Don't feel as though you have to rush right off to your honeymoon. You'll have a much better first day in paradise if you get a good night's sleep in your wedding city first.

5 have a plane plan

If your trip is longer than four hours, bring face cream on board and apply it every hour or so to combat dry skin. For added beauty insurance, tote a refreshing jet pack along for the ride, packed with a toothbrush and toothpaste, face cleanser, hand lotion, a disposable razor, and Tylenol. To keep things simple, only bring the essentials and use small portable containers that are nonspillable and nonbreakable.

Other optional bring-alongs include contact lens solution, ChapStick, an eye pillow, a nail file, a head and neck pillow, a small blanket or wrap, slippers, Visine, sunglasses, and a baseball cap. And if you're traveling from a cold climate to a warm one (or vice versa), don't forget to stash a weather-appropriate change of clothes in your carry-on as well.

6 long layover?

If there's a long layover, find out whether you can check in to the airline's special airport clubs, where you'll likely find cushy lounge areas, waiter service, free Wi-Fi, and more.

7 don't forget

Look up the current exchange rate (if you're traveling to a foreign country) right before you leave, and make sure you have traveler's checks and/or your ATM card; your ID, passports, and other necessary paperwork; your camera and memory cards; comfortable shoes; dress-up clothes; swimsuits and flip-flops; and birth control pills or other medication.

8 download a few shortcuts
Don't even think about going to a boring chain restaurant. Research your options with an international dining app (Zagat has a good one). If you're traveling abroad, put a currency calculator on your phone and download a language converter app too.

9 which name for passports?
The bride's ticket, passport, and all other ID should be in her maiden name; if there are discrepancies, you could run into trouble in customs.

10 make friends
Sure, your honeymoon will be romantic with just the two of you, but it can also make for a boring photo album if you end up with a series of solo "his" and "her" shots. This is your honeymoon, so you want plenty of duo action caught on film. It may seem awkward, but force yourself to ask someone—even if you don't think the person speaks English—to take your photo.

top tips for booking online

Skipping the agent route and booking it yourself?
A few good-to-know tips can go a long way.

1 tuesdays are the cheapest days to buy plane tickets
Travel websites and airlines book more flights on the weekends, so those are the times fares tend to be priciest. Plan to buy your tickets midweek (Tuesdays and Wednesdays are usually best) for the best deals.

2 fly on a tuesday or wednesday
Flights are priciest at the beginning and end of each week when business travelers are making their way to and from home. Plan your itinerary so that you leave midweek and you're bound to find some airline deals.

3 read the fine print
Airline and travel regulations are ever-changing. Read through that annoyingly small print to make sure you're not going to incur any huge hidden fees along the way.

4 use your miles
Sign up for an awards program through your credit card to start collecting airline miles. You just might be able to get one or both of those flights for free!

honeymoon itinerary

Day 1 _____

Day 2 _____

Day 3 _____

Day 4 _____

Day 5 _____

Day 6 _____

Day 7 _____

Day 8 _____

Day 9 _____

Day 10 _____

Day 11 _____

Day 12 _____

Day 13 _____

Day 14 _____

honeymoon contact
cheat sheet

honeymoon destination
_____

tourism bureau number
_____

u.s. embassy number (if abroad)
_____

resort or hotel #1
_____

contact
_____

website
_____

address
_____

phone
_____

resort or hotel #2
_____

contact
_____

website
_____

address
_____

phone
_____

resort or hotel #3
_____

contact
_____

website
_____

address
_____

phone
_____

airline   flight numbers
_____

toll-free number
_____

travel dates   /   /   to   /   /
_____

airline   flight numbers
_____

toll-free number
_____

travel dates   /   /   to   /   /
_____

notes
_____

_____

_____

travel agent

e-mail
_____

website
_____

phone
_____

emergency toll-free number
_____

_____

booking the honeymoon

- ☐ Make hotel and air or train reservations (or have your travel agent arrange them). Ask about using frequent-flier miles and/or special honeymoon hotel packages.

- ☐ If necessary, get passports and ask the tourism bureau or your travel agent if you'll need other travel documents, such as visas.

- ☐ If your destination requires you to get immunizations, do so ASAP.

- ☐ Finalize or confirm travel and hotel reservations.

- ☐ Print out a copy of your itinerary and give it to close family and friends.

notes

techy honeymoon shortcuts

Your wedding day is over! Sit back and relax with apps for your honeymoon.

talktome pro

In a crunch and don't know how to ask, "Where is the nearest bathroom?" in German? Type what you need to say into your phone and this Android app will say it back to you in the selected language.

currency

This handy app will tell you conversion rates for more than 100 currencies. Use it to tip or to calculate how much those cute flats from China cost in U.S. dollars.

postman

Snap a photo, add a greeting, and send a postcard from your iPhone. Share (and brag about) every beautiful beach you lounge on during your honeymoon.

google maps

You're in a foreign country and don't know how to navigate from point A to point B; Google Maps is a must-have. Available on any phone with Internet capabilities, the app lets you search for places, get directions, or just figure out where the heck you are.

weatherbug

It's nice to know the weather forecast when you're traveling, whether you're planning to sunbathe on the beach or spend the day white-water rafting down a river.

triplt

It's inevitable—the info for your flight and hotel always gets buried in your in-box. TripIt consolidates all your trip details, giving you a complete itinerary without any of the hassle.

zagat to go

It's your honeymoon. Don't end up at a boring chain restaurant. Instead, research your dining options—with or without the Internet—using Zagat's app.

wedding budget tracker

Here's a list of every wedding- and honeymoon-related cost we could think of. Try your best to keep track of your expenses as you go along so you aren't shocked when the credit card bills arrive post-honeymoon. Use the general estimates from page 35 to start filling in the first column. Keep track of everything here online at **TheKnot.com/budgeter** (and download the The Knot Planner app so you can update on the go).

wedding service/product	amount budgeted	actual cost
ceremony	$	$
site fee	$	$
officiant fee	$	$
marriage certificate	$	$
programs	$	$
huppah	$	$
candles	$	$
aisle runner	$	$
ring pillow	$	$
other	$	$
reception	$	$
site fee	$	$
rentals	$	$
tent	$	$
tables and chairs	$	$
linens and dinnerware	$	$
dance floor	$	$
portable toilets	$	$

wedding service/product	amount budgeted	actual cost
delivery and setup fees	$	$
other	$	$
food	$	$
service	$	$
beverages	$	$
bartender(s)	$	$
cake	$	$
cutting fee	$	$
delivery fee	$	$
bride's attire	$	$
wedding dress	$	$
alterations	$	$
cleaning	$	$
headpiece and veil	$	$
accessories	$	$
lingerie	$	$
shoes	$	$
gloves	$	$
purse	$	$
other	$	$
hair	$	$
makeup	$	$
manicure(s)	$	$
pedicure(s)	$	$
facial	$	$
massage(s)	$	$

wedding service/product	amount budgeted	actual cost
groom's suit or tux	$	$
shirt	$	$
tie	$	$
vest or cummerbund	$	$
shoes	$	$
cuff links and studs	$	$
groom's grooming	$	$
other	$	$
stationery	$	$
save-the-dates	$	$
invitations and envelopes	$	$
enclosures	$	$
reception invitations	$	$
response cards	$	$
maps	$	$
other	$	$
calligraphy	$	$
postage	$	$
announcements	$	$
thank-you notes	$	$
married stationery	$	$
other	$	$
flowers and décor	$	$
bridal bouquet	$	$
bridesmaid bouquets	$	$
boutonnieres	$	$

wedding service/product	amount budgeted	actual cost
flower girl's flowers	$	$
corsages	$	$
ceremony site arrangements	$	$
centerpieces	$	$
reception site arrangements	$	$
delivery fees and setup	$	$
prop rental(s)	$	$
other	$	$
music/entertainment	$	$
ceremony musicians	$	$
cocktail-hour musicians	$	$
reception band or dj	$	$
children's entertainment	$	$
other	$	$
photo/video	$	$
photography package	$	$
videography package	$	$
additional prints or albums	$	$
additional videos	$	$
rings/jewelry	$	$
bride's ring	$	$
groom's ring	$	$
engraving	$	$
other	$	$

wedding service/product	amount budgeted	actual cost
transportation	$	$
limousine or car rental	$	$
guest shuttle or parking	$	$
hotel room(s)	$	$
welcome bags	$	$
other	$	$
gifts	$	$
attendants	$	$
parents	$	$
party hosts	$	$
each other	$	$
guest favors	$	$
other	$	$
honeymoon	$	$
transportation	$	$
accommodations	$	$
new clothes or gear	$	$
memory cards or film	$	$
sunscreen	$	$
spending money	$	$
other	$	$
marriage license	$	$
blood tests	$	$
other	$	$
tips, taxes, overages	$	$
GRAND TOTAL	$	$

guest list

Here's some space to start making a list of potential guests—all the family members, friends, and colleagues you'd like at your wedding. You can make the official list later—just use this space to jot down names whenever you think of them. Start with the people you're sure about, and end with the "maybes."

1	27
2	28
3	29
4	30
5	31
6	32
7	33
8	34
9	35
10	36
11	37
12	38
13	39
14	40
15	41
16	42
17	43
18	44
19	45
20	46
21	47
22	48
23	49
24	50
25	51
26	52

(CONTINUES)

GUEST LIST (CONTINUED)

53 _____ 87 _____

54 _____ 88 _____

55 _____ 89 _____

56 _____ 90 _____

57 _____ 91 _____

58 _____ 92 _____

59 _____ 93 _____

60 _____ 94 _____

61 _____ 95 _____

62 _____ 96 _____

63 _____ 97 _____

64 _____ 98 _____

65 _____ 99 _____

66 _____ 100 _____

67 _____ 101 _____

68 _____ 102 _____

69 _____ 103 _____

70 _____ 104 _____

71 _____ 105 _____

72 _____ 106 _____

73 _____ 107 _____

74 _____ 108 _____

75 _____ 109 _____

76 _____ 110 _____

77 _____ 111 _____

78 _____ 112 _____

79 _____ 113 _____

80 _____ 114 _____

81 _____ 115 _____

82 _____ 116 _____

83 _____ 117 _____

84 _____ 118 _____

85 _____ 119 _____

86 _____ 120 _____

121 _____

122 _____

123 _____

124 _____

125 _____

126 _____

127 _____

128 _____

129 _____

130 _____

131 _____

132 _____

133 _____

134 _____

135 _____

136 _____

137 _____

138 _____

139 _____

140 _____

141 _____

142 _____

143 _____

144 _____

145 _____

146 _____

147 _____

148 _____

149 _____

150 _____

151 _____

152 _____

153 _____

154 _____

155 _____

156 _____

157 _____

158 _____

159 _____

160 _____

161 _____

162 _____

163 _____

164 _____

165 _____

166 _____

167 _____

168 _____

169 _____

170 _____

171 _____

172 _____

173 _____

174 _____

175 _____

176 _____

177 _____

178 _____

179 _____

180 _____

181 _____

182 _____

183 _____

184 _____

185 _____

186 _____

187 _____

188 _____

189 _____

190 _____

your seating chart

As RSVPs start to roll in, add your guests' names to the list. Hint: You can create
and manage your guest list and seating chart all online at **TheKnot.com/seatingchart.**

table 1

_____
_____
_____
_____
_____
_____
_____

table 3

_____
_____
_____
_____
_____
_____
_____

table 5

_____
_____
_____
_____
_____
_____
_____

table 2

_____
_____
_____
_____
_____
_____
_____

table 4

_____
_____
_____
_____
_____
_____
_____

table 6

_____
_____
_____
_____
_____
_____
_____

table 7

_____
_____
_____
_____
_____
_____
_____

table 10

_____
_____
_____
_____
_____
_____
_____

table 13

_____
_____
_____
_____
_____
_____
_____

table 8

_____
_____
_____
_____
_____
_____
_____

table 11

_____
_____
_____
_____
_____
_____
_____

table 14

_____
_____
_____
_____
_____
_____
_____

table 9

_____
_____
_____
_____
_____
_____
_____

table 12

_____
_____
_____
_____
_____
_____
_____

table 15

_____
_____
_____
_____
_____
_____
_____

gift log

guest's name	gift	thank-you sent
		/ /
		/ /
		/ /
		/ /
		/ /
		/ /
		/ /
		/ /
		/ /
		/ /
		/ /
		/ /
		/ /
		/ /
		/ /
		/ /
		/ /
		/ /
		/ /
		/ /
		/ /
		/ /
		/ /
		/ /
		/ /

guest's name	gift	thank-you sent
		/ /
		/ /
		/ /
		/ /
		/ /
		/ /
		/ /
		/ /
		/ /
		/ /
		/ /
		/ /
		/ /
		/ /
		/ /
		/ /
		/ /
		/ /
		/ /
		/ /
		/ /
		/ /
		/ /
		/ /

photo credits

Special thanks to our photographers:

12: David & Amy Lau Photography

13: Elizabeth Messina

16: Chenin Boutwell Photography

20: 1. Art Beauty Life: Jenny Ebert Photography

21: Elizabeth Messina

33: Marni Rothschild Pictures

37: Gruber Photographers

41: Samuel Lippke Studios

49: La Vie Photography

61: Jonathan Canlas Photography

65: Jamie Hammond Photography

69: Creative Heirloom Photography

75: Heather Cook Elliott Photography

79: Jen Kroll Photography

87: James Christianson Photographers

93: Millie Holloman Photography

95: Nadia D. Photography

105: Atlas Wedding Photography

109: Katelyn James Photography

113: Art Pinney Photography

121: Alison Conklin Photography

128: Michelle Walker Photography

135: Jesse Leake Photography

141: Christian Oth Studio

145: Riverbend Studio

151: Bright Bird Photography

157: Lauren Larsen Photographs

165: Heather Saunders Photography

167: Scott Andrew Studio

173: Elizabeth Messina

181: Brand X/Jupiterimages

index